Still Standing

Still Standing

A Survivor's Story

Hope Concordia M.A., BSW

BALBOA.
PRESS

A DIVISION OF HAY HOUSE

Balboa Press books may be ordered through booksellers or by contacting:

Balboa Press
A Division of Hay House
1663 Liberty Drive
Bloomington, IN 47403
www.balboapress.com
1 (877) 407-4847

Because of the dynamic nature of the Internet, any web addresses or links contained in this book may have changed since publication and may no longer be valid. The views expressed in this work are solely those of the author and do not necessarily reflect the views of the publisher, and the publisher hereby disclaims any responsibility for them.

The author of this book does not dispense medical advice or prescribe the use of any technique as a form of treatment for physical, emotional, or medical problems without the advice of a physician, either directly or indirectly. The intent of the author is only to offer information of a general nature to help you in your quest for emotional and spiritual well-being. In the event you use any of the information in this book for yourself, which is your constitutional right, the author and the publisher assume no responsibility for your actions.

Identifying characteristics in this book have been omitted for traditional privacy reasons. Particular situations have been combined for clarity.

Any people depicted in stock imagery provided by Thinkstock are models, and such images are being used for illustrative purposes only. Certain stock imagery © Thinkstock.

Printed in the United States of America.

ISBN: 978-1-4525-8501-7 (sc)
ISBN: 978-1-4525-8502-4 (e)

Balboa Press rev. date: 11/14/2013

For my beautiful children …

Always remember who you are … magnificent, powerful, worthy, kind, compassionate, loving, forgiving, unstoppable children of light.

Namaste and all of my love!
Mama

For my siblings …

Always remember, love should never hurt.

Foreword

I believe we choose our parents while we are in spirit form in order to learn life's lessons. I also believe that Hope chose to come into this lifetime with two parents who would commit multiple acts of violence and neglect so that she would be able to best serve as a source of light to others. On her soul's journey, Hope endured torturous acts of violence in order to be able to authentically advocate for victims of crime.

Through my own survival and with my career with Laura's House, I have met many diverse victims and survivors. I have seen the effects of child abuse and domestic violence firsthand. I have heard many stories, watched the scars heal and the bruises fade, and witnessed broken bones mend, but Hope's survivor story is different! What makes Hope's survivor story unique is that she first experienced abuse while still inside her mother's womb. She was conceived in darkness and led into more darkness by others who would abuse and manipulate her. Some survivors blame others but not Hope—she has survived without blame and radiates grace and dignity.

Still Standing is an inspirational and multifaceted story that has parts I am familiar with, parts I have heard in my travels, parts I have observed in others, and parts I have been made aware of by colleagues, friends, and family, but I was not aware that all these separate terrors could actually happen to one person. I had no idea that one individual could endure such horrific abuse and yet break the cycle of violence and be brave enough to tell her story. Hope exemplifies resiliency tenfold.

Still Standing is familiar yet unfathomable. This story must not be kept silent; it must be told. Hope's will to survive is astounding! She has broken the cycle of violence in her family and continues to advocate and volunteer with battered men, women, and children. She is educated in the "red flags" of an abuser and knows why victims stay and why abusers abuse. Through all her life lessons, Hope has acquired an abundant supply of passion, empathy, and compassion.

When we blame a victim of domestic violence, rape, sexual assault, or dating abuse, we forget that we have a *victim. Still Standing* will speak to survivors, family, friends, and experts. It will force others to face the truth and to act. I will add *Still Standing* to the California state-mandated Forty-Hour Domestic Violence Advocate Training curriculum, and I will look at it as a reminder that the silence is over and that it is indeed possible to live in harmony after enduring a lifetime of trauma. I am glad Hope is still standing, because many are not. This is an inspiring story about the capacity of one girl's super-human spirit!

Marissa C. Presley

Prevention Education Specialist
Laura's House
999 Corporate Drive, Suite 225
Ladera Ranch, CA 92694
"Ending the Silence of Domestic Violence"
Take the Pledge: www.laurashouse.org/lhteen

Preface

Years ago, an agent of mine named Bonnie Liedtke asked me to write a book. She knew I was a homeless child who made it in the fashion world, and Bonnie thought my story was inspirational. But there was more to my story than "street kid to cover girl." I was too ashamed to tell her about all of the abuse I endured in my youth and in my career and was still enduring in my relationship, so I filed away her idea of sharing my story in print. I trusted that if I was to ever disclose the unspeakable, the universe would reveal the divine time to unveil my facade of normalcy and display the terror of my existence for all to see. That time finally arrived when I was a mother in my late thirties, sitting in Laura's House Domestic Violence Shelter. For once in my life, I was safe. And I began to write this book in the shelter that saved my life. Thank you, Bonnie Liedtke, for planting this seed of Hope.

Acknowledgments

Mark S. Kosins, MD—for your courage

Karl J. Gebhard, MD—for your friendship

Edward H. Guillen, MD—for your bravery

David S. Cannom, MD—for saving my life

Terry McKeever, BSN, RN—for taking me under your wing and helping me reach my potential

Elaine Gotro, MS—for teaching me about FROG (fully rely on God)

Peter Allen Hands, Esq.—for your compassionate heart, dedication, and honesty

San Clemente Police Department—for coming to court on my behalf

California Child Support Services—for advocating in court for my children

Pastor Kris DiLeo—for standing beside me through the lengthy judicial journey

Marissa Presley—for encouraging me to write when fear paralyzed my fingers; for educating me on the cycle of domestic violence and providing a platform to share my story at the shelter

Dara Zane Scully—for reminding me to breathe; for lifting me up when I was in the fetal position on the floor and encouraging me to *stand* up; for walking through the fire of hell beside me

Paula Holm Augenstein—for watching the children so I could obtain an education; for believing in me when I did not believe in myself; for always being there when I needed you most

Introduction

What would you do? In retrospect, I know my path was outlined and protected by the universe from which I came. Many thoughts passed through my subconscious, urging me to answer their magnificent call, but fear, lack of better judgment, and not trusting the process delayed my journey. Many seeds have been planted to nurture this story of unfathomable perseverance. It is perfectly correct to assume that articulating words on paper released the bondage by which my spirit was once trapped and set me free from a self-constructed prison, which secluded me from others. My abusers gave me the gift of tapping into a mental nirvana, which is readily available to everyone, even those who are foreign to enduring trauma. Most individuals, however, are unaware this heavenly place exists. In this tranquil land, I found the key to serenity and physical detachment, regardless of my outside circumstances. As Dr. Wayne Dyer always says, "It is impossible to come from nothing and achieve divinity, unless you were divine in the first place." And he was right!

Table of Contents

Beaten before Born

J am the product of an unwanted pregnancy. My parents were never married, and I was conceived in the back of the Normandy Bar in Los Angeles, California. My father was an AWOL marine, drowning in addiction; my mother was a divorced, pill-popping psychotic. It was a match made so far away from heaven that God himself had to protect me.

My father kicked my mother in the stomach when I was in her womb. He did not want me because I was not a boy—or that is how the story goes. Both parents did the best they could with what they had. This is not a story about blame. I believe that there are no victims in situations, only lessons one needs to learn in order to reach one's individual calling. My parents simply had other priorities than raising a daughter.

I believe we choose our parents to fulfill our soul's journey as we incarnate into this universe. I know now that it is my destiny to help others who were raised in manure to blossom into the most beautiful flowers, by encouraging them to "honor the place inside their spirit, where the entire universe dwells" (Ram Dass).

Pediatric Suicide Failure

*M*y earliest memories are those filled with violence. If I close my eyes and concentrate now, I can still hear my mother's piercing screams as my father strangles her. But I never understood why she would urinate on the floor, suck her thumb, or blow her nose in my father's beer. Are everyone's parents like this? My mom hated me. I think it was because I reminded her of my father. I look a lot like him, and perhaps that was too much for her. She would chase me with a wire hanger, trying to beat me, and scream horrific obscenities until I cried. She would laugh when my tears would fall and tell me she would dance on my grave when I died. I was five years old when I first tried to commit suicide. If this was what life was all about, I knew then I wanted no part of it. I ate an entire bottle of my grandmother's prescription heart medication, but they rushed me to the hospital, pumped my stomach, and then released me back into hell. When I got "home," I remembered seeing a commercial for Fanciful perfume. It warned parents about the dangers of accidental consumption in children, so I drank it. Back to the hospital I went. Why were they saving me?

My mother never said "I love you." When I would ask her if she loved me, she would only say, "What are you? Fucking stupid? You know the answer to that question." I still do not know if she ever loved me. I think she was incapable of loving another human being because she did not love herself.

I grew up living in various motels. My parents paid rent by the week—or should I say, they agreed to pay rent. We would stay there until we got kicked out. I remember selling candy bars to raise money for a school fund-raiser. I would go out on my own, door-to-door, and spend hours trying to raise money. The principal of the school awarded me a nice stereo system for my efforts, but my parents gave it to the motel owner for a week's rent. Most of the motels were infested with roaches, so we had to sleep with the lights on. To be "trailer trash" would have been a step up—I thought it would have been an ideal identity; at least they had a home. I could only wish for a place to call home. We never stayed anywhere long enough to feel settled or secure. I changed schools at least twice a year and imagined what life would be like if I had been born into another family.

My dad always had girlfriends. (Didn't all dads?) When I was five, I remember my dad leaving me with one of them. She was tall, skinny, had "big hair," and drooled a lot. There was a pool in the courtyard, and she asked me if I wanted to swim. I told her I did not know how to swim without a life jacket. She picked me up and threw me in the pool anyway. I screamed and struggled to stay afloat. I watched her put a tube of toothpaste in her mouth with the cap on as she sat cross-legged on the cement, laughing as I gasped for air. I could not understand why she would not help me. She seemed really tired, because she fell asleep while I was drowning. My dad found me in the pool. He'd gone to the motel office to buy cigarettes instead of going to the liquor store. When he got me out of the water, the woman was still asleep next to the pool. I stared at her and cried, while holding on to my dad, but she would not wake up. My dad put me down and went over to her. I watched as he screamed bad words, and she slowly woke up, all smiles. He called her a junkie and said she could have waited a few minutes, until he got back, for a fix.

Sometimes my father would be passed out, naked on a rollaway bed with a jar of Vaseline, and this would infuriate my mother. She said she wondered if he was dead and would call the police to check. He was alive, just drunk and humiliated.

Waking Up Blind

O ne day, I walked to the liquor store with my father. This was a big day for me, because he was going to introduce me to the owner of the liquor store—this was so when he needed cigarettes or beer, I could walk in there with a note from my father and pick them up for him, like any other five-year-old. When we were at the intersection, getting ready to cross the street, I looked at the world around me. I wondered why we did not have a car and always had to walk everywhere. I waited beside my father until the light turned green, and when it did, we began to cross the street. He told me to run. I wanted to please him and ran as fast as I could through the intersection, but I fell and hit my head on the curb. I can still see the yellow Volkswagen Bug that was trying to turn right but could not, because I was lying on the pavement.

A few weeks later, when my mother tried to wake me up for school, my eyes were crossed. My fall had damaged my occipital lobe, which controls sight. I remember her screaming at my father that it was his fault and that when I grew up, nobody would ever want me. She said if he had not been drunk that night, my eyes would be okay and I could have had a chance.

My mother took me to the welfare office. We sat in a large room on cold metal chairs for hours, until they called her name. An old woman called us into her office, and she looked at me with pity. I hated the feeling I had inside my stomach when she smiled at me out of duty. She told us it was such a shame about my eyes, and then she told me not to worry; her company would pay for me to see a doctor. They gave my mother "stickers" that would pay for my medical expenses. I walked out of there, understanding why children at school had sticker collections. I had two eye operations before my seventh birthday. I was in the hospital about five days each time. My mother never stayed with me. My father stayed once.

The nurses told me I could not eat anything after they gave me a shot, but my father snuck in a Dr. Pepper and a Hershey's chocolate bar. As I ate my reward for being brave, the nurse returned and was upset with my father. She took away my snacks and told me I had to get another shot because I'd eaten when I was not supposed to. I looked at my father and began to cry. I did not want another shot. I hated shots and fought them every step of the way. Several nurses had to hold me down, and they asked my father to leave the room. I was alone and scared. When my father returned, he handed me a Barbie doll. This was the first and only toy he ever gave me. My grandmother stayed with me for the second operation. She would push me in the wheelchair up and down the halls. There was a playroom for sick children, and we would spend hours in there together.

During my stay at the hospital, I had my own room; I had food and clean pajamas. There was no yelling, hitting, or bad words. The nurses even had a party for me and gave me presents when I was discharged from the hospital. I felt so special there. I wished I could have stayed there forever.

Innocence Lost

ometimes my mom and dad would become managers at an apartment building to get free rent. It never lasted long, though, and we would always end up back in a motel.

My parents told me not to go into anyone's house if there were not any adults at home, but I did anyway. I made a friend who was five, just like me. She had an older brother who was home from jail, so I thought he was old enough to be the "adult." My friend and I began to play doctor. We kissed, and I liked the way it felt. Her brother saw us and told us to play in the living room. He sat at the kitchen table, sharpening a big knife with a black handle. He was smiling oddly and then told us to walk toward him. He asked us what we were doing, and we giggled. He put the knife to my throat and told me to take off my clothes. I did—I was scared. I stood there, naked, and obeyed him. I do not remember what happened, but I do remember running home, screaming, without clothes. My parents told me it was my fault, because I'd gone into someone's house when her mom and dad were not at home. They yelled at me and called the police.

Two officers stood in my bedroom as I tried to hide and become invisible. They asked me questions. I thought I was going to get in trouble for playing doctor, so I lied and said we did not kiss. The officers left, and I went back to the hospital. I remember having to meet with one doctor on a regular basis after I was discharged again. We would play board games on the grass outside the hospital on sunny days, or I would draw pictures inside the office if it was cold outside. The doctors and nurses were so nice; I wished my parents liked me as much as they did.

Will Work for Food

*G*oing to the grocery store was such a treat. I loved walking up and down the huge aisles, watching mothers push their children in the shopping carts filled with food. I would imagine that I was one of their children, and I'd stand up a little taller with the idea. I noticed one of the markets tried to encourage shoppers to return the carts after they loaded the groceries into the car, instead of leaving the carts in open parking spaces. They gave "stickers" to the shoppers who returned their shopping carts, which could be saved in a book and redeemed on their next visit for food. I decided to collect the carts myself and bring groceries home for my family. I would stay at the parking lot alone—all day on weekends and after school—until it got dark. I would go up to people and offer to return their cart, and then I'd collect the stickers. After working for hours, dreaming of a nice meal, I found out I was only able to get one free stick of butter. I hated butter. I asked if I could please have some milk or a candy bar, but cashier said no. Still, I had my first job at the ripe old age of six.

By this time, I now had a baby sister and baby brother. I am five years older than my sister and six years older than my brother. But I was the one in charge of raising them. By the time I was seven years old, I would be dropped off at a mall for hours, with both children. I would not have any money, diaper bags, or even a stroller. As my mother would leave the store, I would beg her not to make me watch them, because the children would cry when they were hungry, and I could not feed them. They would run in different directions, and I could not always catch them, and people would stare at us.

One time, my mom dropped us off and laughed at me when I begged her not to leave. She told me to meet her in the Sears toy department at five o'clock. The store had just opened for the day, so I knew it was ten o'clock in the morning. I did not have a watch—I couldn't tell time anyway—but she told me to ask strangers for the time. I had seen the news and heard of kidnappers that had killed some children. I asked my mom how she could leave us there; what if someone kidnapped us? She laughed as she walked away, and with her back to us, she said, "No one will ever take you. Nobody wants you." The hours never seemed to pass. I saw a woman who was demonstrating new nonstick cookware; she was making eggs. I watched her as I held one baby on my hip and the other by the hand. She asked me questions about my parents, and I made up stories of what I thought was normal and what she wanted to hear.

Weekend after weekend, I would stand and watch her cook, and she would feed us. I think she knew that we were hungry, and there were never any adults with us. She would watch me, taking care of the children, out of the corners of her eyes, as she tried to sell the newest nonstick pans. I became fond of her. She was gentle, and she smiled as she fed us. I wished she would take us home with her.

On other weekends, especially during the summer, we three kids would be dropped off at a park or public swimming pool. We would stay there from sunup to sundown, even if it was raining. I would check the public telephones or the newspaper coin returns for money. I was always blessed to find some. It was as if the universe provided for our needs. On most days, I would find three quarters. The ice cream man sold things that cost forty-five cents. He would see my troubled face, and say, "Kid, what do you want?" When I told him how much money I had, he would always give me three push-ups, one for each of us. I felt so lucky. I needed to feed my hungry brother and sister, but I was hungry too.

When we were at the public swimming pool, I did not have much luck. They had vending machines, and the machine could not sympathize with the eyes of three hungry children. I usually bought one small can of chili. It was not enough for one person, let alone three, so I would take only one small bite and then feed my brother and sister the rest. I can still feel the warm sensation and satisfaction I felt for providing food for them. That one bite did not fill my belly, but it did take the chill off from the cold rain. I never understood why the public pool was open on rainy days. I hated being dropped off there during a storm. It was so difficult to keep my brother and sister warm, fed, and happy when I had no money, and we were outside in the cold.

Crime and Cotton Candy

*A*t a store called Gemco and at another one called Zody's, my mother taught me how to switch tickets on items to get them for less money. She would take me into these really big stores that sold food and clothes and have me try on beautiful dresses. I loved the way I felt when I was wearing nice clothes. I rarely was able to take them home, but if only for a moment in the dressing room, all was normal in my reflection. I would watch her peel off price tags and replace them with other ones. Sometimes, she would give me the tags she wanted switched and tell me where to put them. I wanted her to love me, so I did what she asked. I must have got really good at it, because I started getting new school clothes—really new, not from thrift stores.

Then she upped the ante. She would have me go into a store and find the coffee pots, grab one, and take it to the counter, telling the cashier that I had to return it. If the cashier asked me where my parents were, I was told to say that my mom was waiting for me in the car. We did not have a car. If I convinced the cashier to give me the money, I would be able to go to Disneyland!

I went to Disneyland three times. As I walked down Main Street, I wondered if the other children around me had to switch tickets in order to be there too. I asked my mother, and she told me to shut up and never tell anyone, or she could get in trouble and I would never get anything nice again.

Just Another Day

*M*y mom would sell towels that she'd stolen from the motel. I never understood why anyone would want them. They were white, thin, and scratchy. They smelled of bleach, and my body would get bumps and itch after I used them.

I remember one customer, an elderly woman named Delores. She was black, in a wheelchair, and I think she was a pharmacist, because my mother would leave with pills to make her relax. They would tell me to wait in the living room and watch television while they did "business." One day when we went over to sell her towels, I saw a man who was strapped to a chair in restraints, naked and screaming. Delores said it was her son and told me not to pay attention to him.

There were a lot of people in the house and a lot of crying. I think someone died. I remember hearing that one of her children was going to be buried in a red Corvette. Music was playing really loud, and I thought it was an odd party.

Daddy's Dancing Daughter

My dad would drink beer and ask me to dance for him. I wanted him to love me, so I danced as he drank and smoked in the chair that sat beside the broken table in the dirty motel room. He would smile at me when I would roll around on the floor. I knew he liked watching me, so I kept giving him his show. Sometimes, when I would get tired, he would throw tennis balls at me if I stopped. I felt like I was at the batting cages, and I was the target. My mom would yell at him when she would see me dancing. My dad was hardly ever at the motel; he was always with his girlfriends or at the strip club. I thought if I danced for him, at least he would be "home."

I got my first hickey from my father when he was drunk. I remember my friends at school asking me what was on my neck as we rode on the school bus. I did not know what to say. I made up a lie. I was now the hero among the group of children for the day. The girls all wanted to know what it felt like, and the boys all stared and giggled. How could I tell them the truth? How could I tell anyone?

There's No Escape

*M*y parents decided a new state would fix their problems, so we went to Reno. My father's family lived there. I had never met my dad's family, but we were going to live with my grandmother until we found another motel and my parents got jobs. It was nice to be in a house. His mother was a retired nurse and was divorced from his father. I heard them talk about the "drunk" but never understood why they would call his father names. My dad has five brothers and a sister, and all of them drank beer until they fell asleep in odd places. My mother got into a fight with my dad's sister, and someone pulled a knife and tried to stab someone in the TV room, so we had move again.

This time we went to a motel that gave us free doughnuts in the morning, so at least I knew we would have something to eat. At night, my mother would take my sister, my brother, and me to the Gospel Mission to eat dinner. We would line up outside with all of the other homeless men, women, and children and wait for two hours before they served the meal, just to make sure we would get fed.

I really liked the Gospel Mission. They had us sing praise songs before they let us eat. I remember standing on the stage, singing "Amazing Grace," and feeling so safe. They always let the women and children eat before the men. I wished we could all eat together. I would look over and see men in the pews, waiting for us to finish so they could be served. They were so patient and so quiet. Although they smelled really bad, I was not afraid of them. I wondered how they ended up there and if they had families. I wanted to help them and make them smile. I would sing praise songs and attempt eye contact with them, and this made me feel like I was doing something good for their souls.

After singing one night, I walked off the stage and toward the kitchen, passing the pews filled with hungry men. A homeless man asked me what I was doing at the mission and told me I did not belong there. I felt so sad. I never belonged anywhere. When he saw my face, he said, "Kid, nobody belongs here," and smiled. His smile invigorated me with hope. I wondered when he'd smiled last and if he would smile at me again, even though his words caused me pain.

Please Keep Me!

$\mathcal{M}$y grandma on my mother's side loved me, or so I thought, until she drove me to Orangewood Children's Home. She walked me into this beautiful building in Costa Mesa, which was down the street from her apartment. The woman at the front desk told us that the courts needed to send a child to this place, and she could not just check me in like luggage. I did not understand why my grandma did not want me to stay with her anymore. Had I done something wrong? Did I eat too much? Did I say something I should not have? Why was she tired of me? Was I boring? I put my head down as the lady explained that my grandmother would have to take me home with her.

I felt so empty inside and totally alone. Orangewood seemed like a beautiful place to live, but I was not wanted there either. So off I went, back to my grandma's, and we never spoke of it again. Years later, I found myself, as an adult woman, volunteering with a particular organization, which required me to take a tour of Orangewood. I was nervous as I walked through the facility. I kept wondering if they would remember me.

As I walked through the huge, beautiful grounds, I saw clean rooms, with adorable racecar beds. They had a large kitchen and a beautiful picnic-style dining area. It is what I would imagine a summer camp looked like. Those lucky enough to be welcomed into this home were able to eat every day. How refreshing to have food and not be hit, spit on, chased, or cussed at while they stayed there. They even had a playroom with a lot of toys. There, an unwanted child could actually be free and be normal. I wished again that they would have taken me.

As our tour bus pulled away, we went on our way to our next philanthropic venue. The other philanthropists were chatting about additions to their homes, plans for dinner, and vacation destinations, while I sat quietly, reflecting on my experience and trying not to cry. I pretended to smile and passively engage in conversation. Would the women like me, if they knew I was just like the kids in that place? Would they look at me differently if they knew I was not like most of them?

I found myself questioning why I'd chosen to join such a prestigious group of volunteer women. They came from a different world than mine, filled with trust funds, houses in the Hamptons, and leisure lunches. I felt like a fraud. Did I even belong with those ladies? Who was I trying to fool? I always pretended I came from a normal family, and I lived in the land of make-believe. I cherished what others took for granted or complained about—overprotective father and smothering mother? Sign me up!

The Boogeyman is Real

I remember a time when my sister was about two and my dad was giving her a bath. I needed to go to the bathroom, so I opened the door, and he was sitting on the side of the tub, drunk, staring at her. She was sitting in about two inches of water, not smiling or making a sound. She stared at me. I felt weird in my stomach and walked out. My mom saw my face and walked into the bathroom and began to scream.

She ran outside, and I chased after her. I fell down a step, and I cried, "Mommy, wait!" She did not stop. I ran after her into the street, between the cars. When I caught up to her, she pulled some money out of her bra and said we were going to sleep in another motel that night and eat dinner. And we did. We went out to a smorgasbord and ate a lot food and then rented a room for the night. My sister was just a toddler, and my mom left my infant brother with my dad that night too. As I lay in the new motel room, I could not sleep. I kept wondering if my sister and brother were okay. I hoped they had food and were not crying for me. I felt bad that I'd followed my mom. I should have stayed and taken care of them.

～

I hate parks. One time, my mom did not dump me off with the kids; she actually stayed at the park with us. She sat on a bench, and I sat beside her, watching my brother and sister play. A woman joined us who I'd never seen before. I am not sure if my mom knew her, but the woman wanted to buy my sister. The woman asked how much money my mom needed and said she would take my baby sister in exchange. My mom did not say no; she said she would need to ask my dad. I sat there wondering if she was going to sell me next. Would anyone even want to buy me? My mom smiled at me in such a creepy way. I guess my dad said no, because my sister stayed with us.

~

*M*y mom rode the city bus with us. One day, the bus driver paid a particular interest in my brother and offered to take him "off her hands" for the weekend. She did not know this man. She did not even have his phone number or address. But she still said yes. She gave the bus driver the name of our motel, and he came over after his shift. My brother spent the weekend with him. This happened a lot. He would buy my brother expensive gifts and sometimes buy my mom things too. I knew this was not right. I decided to explain what was happening to the school counselor. My mother was so mad at me! She screamed at me, calling me a "fucking jealous bitch," and said I should have kept my mouth shut.

The bus driver's brother was a police officer for the city where we lived. A meeting at the police station was arranged. My mom, the bus driver, my sister, and I attended the meeting. My brother told me the man would kiss him and touch him. I shared this at the meeting in the police station, as I had with the counselor. They all looked at me like I was the crazy one. My brother even said I was telling the truth. I did everything I could to help him. The room was filled with coldness, and my brother was filled with shame. Did I do the wrong thing by violating his trust and trying to protect him? Nothing happened to the bus driver, and he was back at our motel in a matter of weeks. By this time, it was summer, and school was out. My brother's trips would last longer, and I was even more worried about his safety.

~

My mom would visit various churches to get free food. She didn't attend church services; she only went there to talk to the priests and try to manipulate them into giving her what she wanted—money, food, vouchers for thrift stores. I remember being in downtown Los Angeles one winter morning. I sat inside an empty church office—cold, hungry, and alone. The place seemed really big, and it echoed when I would talk. I sat on the floor. I was dirty and did not feel worthy of sitting on the chair. I imagined I was a nun, and I lived there. How wonderful it would be to be a child of God and live in God's house. I bet nothing bad ever happened there.

~

My mom found a couple who wanted to adopt me. They rescued dogs, and now they were going to rescue me too. I was so happy! They had a house and did not hurt me. I lived with them for a while. They'd always wanted children but for medical reasons could not conceive. The woman would take me to the beauty shop and spend time asking me questions about what I want to become when I grew up. She was truly interested in me. I'd never experienced that before. I'd always felt like a burden to my parents.

I offered to clean my new family's house to earn my keep, but they said I just needed to clean my room. Yes, I had a room. A real bed in a real room that was all mine. I was excited to clean it.

I would find myself lying in bed, staring at "my room," admiring it for hours. I would not want to sleep, because I thought maybe when I woke up in the morning, it would all be gone. And then it happened—one morning at breakfast, they told me they were having a baby. They were pregnant—and I was on my way out, again. I thanked them for taking care of me for the short time they did and said their baby was really lucky. I was so sad to go, but changing places is what I did best. Consistency? What is that?

~

When I was ten years old, I watched a teenager—I will call her "Sally"—care for an old man in a wheelchair. I was living in the "apartment du jour" and was their neighbor. I was so excited when she would come outside and tell me about her day. Sally was young and cool. She smoked cigarettes. She didn't go to school. She didn't have parents. Sally had money and seemed to be living the good life. She wore her curly blonde hair tied in ponytail, and she wore high heels, but she never laughed. She would cook and clean for the old man, but she also could eat whatever she wanted and watch any kind of TV shows—and she even had her own room! I wanted to be just like her. I had to get up the courage to ask her if I could help, or if she could give me someone to take care of too.

One day, I was playing in the courtyard when the coroner arrived, and I saw my teenage friend was crying. Sally told me the man she cared for had died that day. I hugged her. I figured she was sad because she would not see him anymore, but I was wrong. Sally was worried about where she would live, how she would eat, and who was going to hurt her next. My teenage friend had the same worries as I did—I felt connected to her. The next morning, Sally was gone too. I never saw her again. I never even knew her real name. She once told me, "My name is anything you want it to be." That night, I prayed to God, asking him to take my life or help me live through this one. I knew that God existed, because there had to be something better out there than the horror all around me.

On My Own

*T*he first time I ran away was different from all the other times—because my grandma helped me. My mom's sister worked with a woman who offered to let me stay with her, and my grandma arranged the details. I was so excited to have another prospective home, but I wondered what it would be like and how long this one would last. Still, it could not be any worse than what I was used to, so I imagined it would be warm, loving, and clean. Somehow, I understood the power of thought and decided to focus on my desires and not what I was escaping.

I never understood why people complained. I could always find joy in the most horrific circumstances. The power of thought proved true again, and the house was much more than I could have ever wanted. The woman and her husband smiled all the time and never yelled or hit me. I had my own room, with a beautiful handmade quilt on the bed that smelled so fresh. I would snuggle up in it and hold on tight. It made me feel so safe. I had my own bathroom, with my own shampoo and conditioner. My first night there, the woman tried to lovingly brush the hair out of my dirty face, and her fingernails got stuck in my hair. She frowned and said, "Poor girl. When was the last time you brushed your hair?" I told her I let my sister, who was in kindergarten, style my hair often. I tried to assure her that it was the latest fashion.

She grimaced and put me in the bath. I kept thinking about her calling me "poor girl." I did not want to be poor. How could she tell? I felt like a puppy in the pound, jumping inside a cage, doing tricks; wishing someone would fall in love with me and take me home—and just keep me already. That particular reprieve from hell only lasted one week. I wished I could have stayed forever, but my grandma said that if I stayed, the kind people would be put in jail for harboring a runaway. Why would the police do that to them? They were protecting me from my drug-addict parents who wished me dead. The woman cried as the officer put me in the back of a police car and sent me back to hell. The officer mumbled, "You don't look like you're being abused. You're clean, and you smile all the time. Life can't be that bad at home."

I was bathed and had on nice clothes but only because the woman who was "harboring" me had given me a bath and bought me new outfits. And as for smiling, I did that all the time to cover up my pain. I would think happy thoughts and force myself to smile. If others believed I was truly happy, I might just believe it myself.

I believe if we can find peace in the midst of chaos, we can transcend into another dimension. I have been on a quest for that place of stillness all of my life. Then—and only then—do we know true freedom from materialistic clutches. It is easy to say "all is well with my soul" when we are not beaten, hungry, or homeless. It is another to actually believe it "will be well" while watching the world violently explode all around us.

I practiced centering myself in the God-realized consciousness and drawing up joy from my heart. Joy is a choice that is not dependent upon outside circumstances. It glows effortlessly from my soul; it always has. Joy is my friend that wiped away my tears and warmed my lonely spirit with its rays of hope. Joy gave me the courage to continuously seek God and realize that I, too, deserve contentment.

I did not stay back at the motel with my parents for long. I made a choice to run away again. But, this time I ran right into danger, drugs, and darkness. I was twelve years old, living on the streets, on top of school roofs, in garages, and in friends' houses. Some drug dealers took me in and gave me a place to sleep. They did not hit me, so it was better than being at the motel with my mom or dad. I saw weird things, like people giving themselves shots under their toenails. Unfortunately, I surrounded myself with the same type of people I'd run away from. I was in an identical environment but in a different location.

I could not stay with the dealers for long either. It was time for me to find a new place to live again. They told me about an abandoned garage and assured me I would have a mat on the floor and a blanket waiting for me. They kept their promise. The floor was cold, but I did not freeze to death. Too bad.

I was scared there and could not sleep. I was afraid someone would open the garage and hurt me for being there. It was so dark that I could not see my hand in front of my face. I worried about rats crawling on me as I lay down to rest. I wondered if they had big teeth and how it would feel if they bit me. I was used to sleeping with roaches at the motel but not knowing if there were any in the garage also concerned me. I don't like surprises.

I closed my eyes and tried to remember that homemade quilt from a prior adventure. I concentrated on the fresh, clean scent and soft cozy yarn. I pretended I was tucked in bed at the home of my first runaway family. I imagined I was safe, and my body began to relax. I was still in the fetal position on floor, but at least I could breathe now. There was no bathroom. I was too afraid to open the garage door in the middle of the night, so I waited until the morning. When the sun rose, I was still afraid to open the door. When I walked out, I feared people would laugh at me.

I slowly pushed up the door, and I saw a man standing in

the alley. He did not laugh as I'd anticipated; he just stared at me with a puzzled look on his face. I ran away as fast as I could before he could ask me any questions. I ran to the nearest fast-food restaurant, used their restroom, and took a bath in their sink. I shampooed my hair with hand soap and dried it with paper towels. I wished I had clean clothes to put on. I looked into the mirror and pictured myself in a beautiful dress—soft satin and strapless. I imagined that my hair was really long, with curls cascading down my back. I wished I were a princess. If only I had a fairy godmother, life would be so different! If only I had a mother!

I left the restaurant hungry, but at least I was clean. I tried to hold my head up high and quickly exit while people were eating, I felt many of them stare at me. I pretended I had somewhere to go, so I walked even faster toward the door. Although I knew I would just walk aimlessly down the street, I was in a hurry to do so. I thought that acting as if I was really busy would distract them from my homelessness. Their looks of condemnation and disgust pierced my soul. I could not escape the daggers. Why were they so mad at me? I did not even know them. One man yelled, "Hey, girl!" but I ignored him. I was halfway down the street, away from the restaurant, when he called out for the third time, and I turned around. I'd thought no one would be calling me, but I was wrong. He was calling me, holding up a bag. This stranger had bought me breakfast from the restaurant where I'd had my morning bath. I smiled and walked toward him, put my head down, and shook my head. I could not believe someone would care if I ate. This was a new experience. His kindness erased all of the daggers I dodged earlier that morning. He gave me strength to fight for another day. I actually thought, just for a split second, that I was loved by someone.

Homeless and Hungry

*W*hen I was thirteen years old, I realized I needed a job. Fast-food restaurants lined the main boulevard, so I decided that would be a perfect place to begin my search. I entered a Taco Bell and said, "Could I have a job, please?" The cashier asked me if I wanted an application. I was not sure what an application was, so I just stared at her with wide-open eyes. She looked puzzled and told me to wait a minute while she got the manager.

A woman quickly came to the counter and rapidly began asking me questions. She spent about five minutes trying to get to know me, and I thought things were going very well. She offered me the job, and asked me if I could come in the next morning to fill out the paperwork. I told her I had to go school in the morning, but I could come in right after. She said, "Wait a minute—how old are you?" When I told her that I was thirteen, she said I was not old enough; I needed to be sixteen to work there. Everything was perfect—except my age. I was so sad! What was I going to do now?

I decided to go next door to another fast-food place and try again. When I walked up to the counter, a man asked, "May I take your order?" I smiled and said, "Not yet. I need to get a job first. May I have an application?" (Now I knew what an application was.) He passed me a piece of paper, and as I began to read it, the manager approached and introduced himself. We began to discuss the idea of my becoming a cook. I was so happy that he wanted me to work there, but I did not know how to cook. When he asked me how old I was, I lied and said I was sixteen. He asked me several more questions and told me to fill out the application. I sat on the bench next to a family that was eating. I could smell the food. I was so hungry. I wondered if they could hear my stomach growl. I looked around, fantasizing about eating there.

I was so happy to have the opportunity to work. As I walked to the counter to turn in my application, I stood up a little taller and smiled from the inside. I felt so good about myself. The manager began to make small talk and asked me what grade I was in. I answered honestly and said I was in eighth grade. He looked at my application and said, "Wait a minute—it says here that you're sixteen." I did not know what to do. My stomach started to hurt, and I just hung my head and went on to the next place.

I remembered a girl at school who always bragged about having a job that paid her a lot of money. Why did they let her work and not me? What was wrong with me? I saw that girl later that week. She invited me over to her home. She fed me and shared that her mother was married for the third time to a teacher at our school—she said I shouldn't be surprised if I saw our math teacher in her home. She made me promise not to tell anyone. I did not know why it was such a secret, but I said okay. I saw pictures of my friend with the math teacher in the house but none with her mother. As we were sitting in the kitchen, our math teacher came in the front door. I didn't know why, but he made me leave immediately. I heard him whisper, "I told you never to bring anyone over here." I did not have time to ask her about the job. How was I going to eat now?

Later that night I met a new group of homeless kids, who invited me to go "crackering"—street-kid slang for a way of finding something to eat. We went to the nicest hotel in the

45

area and took the elevator to the top floor. We walked the halls, looking for food trays that the guests had placed outside their rooms after ordering room service. Very carefully, we lifted the metal lids off the plates, looking for anything salvageable. I quickly learned that we had to do this quietly and not giggle.

I got excited when I saw a half-eaten dinner in the hall. I laughed out loud, calling for my newfound friends. As they ran down the halls in the direction of my voice, the door to the guest's room opened. I was sitting on the floor beside the tray, picking peas from a crumpled napkin. The man yelled at me, saying he was calling security. We all ran to the elevators, nervously laughing but wondering if security would be waiting for us on the first floor. When the doors opened on the ground level, the lobby was empty. We ran away as fast as we could and never looked back.

Against All Odds

*T*he next day, I tried to find a job again. I walked into Burger King and asked for the manager. If I was too young to work for them too, I did not want to waste time filling out more applications. An older woman with orange-dyed hair and sweet eyes approached the counter. I felt as though I knew her, and it was oddly comfortable. I decided to just tell her the truth—I was a thirteen-year-old homeless kid who went to school and needed a job. She asked me to wait twenty minutes and handed me a hamburger and a drink. I watched her take money out of her pockets and hand it to the cashier to pay for the food. I was so happy! I loved it here already! I kept thinking, "I hope she picks me."

As I ate my burger, I looked around at the environment, trying not to get my hopes up too high. When the woman came over, she asked if she could sit at my table. No one had ever asked permission to join me before. I felt so safe. She asked me about my parents, but I would not say anything about them—I was ashamed. The manager was nice, but I did not trust her—I didn't trust anyone. She told me that when I turned fourteen, I could work for her after school with a permit. I was so happy! I was almost fourteen! She made me promise to stay in school and told me she was looking forward to the day she would give me my uniform. I'd never had a uniform. New clothes sounded like heaven. She told me I would learn how to cook and could eat all of my mistakes. And when I got good at cooking and no longer made mistakes, I could eat whatever I wanted on the menu at half price. What a blessing—a job, food, and a nice person to take care of me. This was the good life. All I had to do was survive on the streets for three more months. I could do that.

~

Behind a local grocery store I found boxes filled with lettuce. I went into the store and asked if I could have the food inside the boxes placed beside the trashcan. The cashier asked me why. "I have to feed my bunny," I said. She spoke into her microphone, paging the manager to her checkout stand. *Ugh*, I thought, *another manager! Managers make all of the decisions. How do I get that job?*

The manager walked over to checkout stand, and the cashier conveyed my request. He looked me up and down and said, "Yeah, I suppose that would be all right." He told me which days he put the old produce beside the trash. He said I should try to pick it up as soon as possible, because he did not want to be responsible if my bunny got sick from eating rotten food. I smiled and crinkled my nose. It was my way of telling him I was the bunny. I don't think he understood me. He mumbled as he hurried away, "How could a kid get so excited over rabbit food?"

~

My fourteenth birthday felt like the best birthday ever, because I finally could get a job. What a wonderful gift! I woke up in a motel room and turned on the clock radio. Tina Turner was singing "What's Love Got to Do with It." I put on an old dress that someone had given me, looked into the mirror, and promised myself that I was going to make it out of hell.

Even at a very young age, I intuitively knew that we are the thoughts we think about. I decided to focus on the things I wanted, and they began to happen. I focused on getting a job, getting off the streets, and finding love. As I looked in the mirror, I saw my feathered hair, gold dangle earrings, and rainbow tiered dress reflected back at me. *I am beautiful. Why don't my parents want me?* I told myself I would not worry about them today; I would just pretend that I was loved. I began to think of all the things for which I was grateful, instead of what I was missing.

Then I realized God always provided for me, even as a homeless child, eating out of trash cans. But why did I have so much pain inside my heart? I really wanted to run away again, but I was already gone. I was trying to escape from myself. I felt like my entire existence was make-believe. I was constantly pretending my life was normal, and it was beyond exhausting. I needed to be alone. I needed to find a place where I could be free to be myself, a place where happiness would bring unlimited possibilities. I knew I had to create my own existence, and I was absolutely positive it was going to be fabulous.

It was official—I was old enough to work at Burger King. As I walked down the street to my fast-food haven, I hoped the manager still worked there and prayed she would keep her promise. I peeked through the window at the place I desperately wanted to call my home. The restaurant was crowded and busy. I saw lines of people, impatiently pacing and shaking their heads, waiting to order, and the trash cans were overflowing. I prayed for the courage to actually walk inside.

After a few moments, I cautiously opened the door. Now I had to gather my courage to speak with someone and ask for the manager. I walked up to the counter and stood beside the line. I wanted to make sure the cashier didn't ask to take my order—that would have been embarrassing, as I didn't have any money. I began to feel tense and resentful. I feared the people in line would hear my stomach growl or sense my jealousy of their being able to buy food. I tried to ignore the imagined judgment of those who were fortunate enough to eat. I channeled all of my negative emotions into strength.

In a squeaky voice filled with timid insecurity, I asked to speak with the manager. Although my voice was soft as a mouse, it reached the ears of my angel in the kitchen. She looked up and smiled at me. "Hope, right? Come on back." At that moment, my life changed. Someone believed in me and actually wanted me. As I walked with a skip in my step to the back of kitchen, I decided, right then and there, that I was going to be the best worker ever. I would go above and beyond my duties to show my gratitude. I would arrive early and stay late—and hope they would never give me away. That reprieve from destitution lasted until the restaurant sold. I wished things could have stayed the same for a little longer, but I was grateful for the time I spent there, learning from my coworkers.

~

Balloons tied to the door of a new frozen yogurt store greeted the patrons waiting for the grand opening. People overflowed the tiny shop, and a line spilled out the door. I wondered why they were so busy. It reminded me of the line to get into Disneyland. Were they giving away free yogurt? I decided to ask someone waiting in line why it was so crowded. "It's the grand opening celebration," a man told me. He was holding a special coupon that allowed each person to get a large cup of frozen yogurt for a quarter. *Where did he get it?* I wondered. I had panhandled a quarter earlier but still needed a coupon. Seconds after I had that thought, the woman standing beside the man gave me her extra coupon. I was so hungry and grateful. My smile was ear to ear as I joined them in line.

As I approached the cashier, the owner noticed my friendly personality—and he offered me a job on the spot! I could not believe it! I accepted and started immediately. Swiftly, I was taken behind the counter and handed a red apron. I wasn't asked to fill out any paperwork, and no one asked about my age or where I lived. I was good enough, at that very moment just as I was. I felt human and equal with mankind. I didn't know how much I would get paid, but I washed my hands, stepped up to the counter, and asked, "How I may serve you?" I quickly learned how to run the yogurt machine, and I felt whole and worthy. That day, I had purpose—but still I wondered how long it would last.

After that day, the owner rarely came to the shop. She and her husband would stop by once a month to empty the safe and check in with the staff. My manager was a woman in her late twenties. I was only fifteen and thought she was so worldly. She had already traveled to another country. She said she'd had a baby but had given it away to a friend. She lived with her mother and sister, but her sister was a heroin addict who was in and out of jail for prostitution.

My manager knew I needed a place to live and offered me her sister's floor. I was so blessed to be out of the cold and was excited to have a place to sleep. Life was good; I had a job, and I had a new home. I felt like God was always taking care of me. I was never on the streets for long. He always put people in my life who would feed me, give me a place to sleep, and offer me jobs.

Screaming in Silence

*I*s a girl's virginity lost when she is molested, or is it the first time she willingly agrees to have sex? I was fifteen and willing. The man—I'll call him Johnny—was twenty-five. He did not work, lived with his parents, carried a gun, and played in a band.

When I met Johnny, he lied about his age and told me he was nineteen. He hung out at local high schools and slept with a lot of teenage girls, who gave him money.

Johnny beat me, strangled me, stabbed me, attempted to run me over with his speeding car, and regularly suffocated my screams with a pillow until I lost consciousness. He did most of this in front of my mother, and she did nothing to help me. I started giving my weekly paychecks to Johnny—I thought I was in love and wanted to please him. I thought, *Johnny would be perfect if he was not so violent all of the time.*

~

*L*ater that same year, a scout from a modeling agency approached me. I was surprised that someone would think I was beautiful. I dressed in black, had purple hair, and my nose was pierced with a safety pin—this façade was an attempt to protect me from other people. The modeling agency scout handed me her card and said, "You have what it takes to make it in the business." She said I could make a lot of money, have apartments anywhere in the world, and could even have my picture in fashion magazines. I was excited at the idea of having a home, and if it had to be in another country, that was just fine with me.

I did not have a car or know how to drive. Johnny forbade me from learning. He assured me he would drive me to all of my auditions if I paid him for gas and provided oral sex in the car as he drove. I was grateful that I would be able to get a ride to Los Angeles. I did not know how I was going to come up with the extra cash for gas, because he already took my entire paycheck. I agreed and secretly focused on the idea of escaping to another land—a land that did not hurt me; a land where I could be just like everyone else; a place where I could work, keep the money I earned, have an apartment, and maybe find someone to love me.

The agency gave me a drastic makeover. I was sent to a Beverly Hills salon to have my hair done. As I looked around at the women sipping tea and champagne, an overwhelming sense of anxiety engulfed me. I was afraid that I did not belong there. I was dirty and terrified that my secret could be exposed any second. I could not help but wonder if any of these women had ever spent the night on the streets or cried themselves to sleep, begging God to take their lives. The hairstylist must have felt my tension, because she said, "This is supposed to be a fun experience. Try to enjoy yourself."

After several hours, the masterpiece was completed. The agency chose my hair color and style, and I no longer recognized the girl in the mirror. She was pretty, soft, and very approachable. My purple hair was gone, and gentle brown tresses framed my face. My inside did not match the outside, however, and I was totally uncomfortable. I felt like vomiting. I was told to go directly to the agency for approval and wardrobe.

Their faces lit up as I entered the room, and I felt the glorious power of aesthetic perfection. They smiled at me and said I was beautiful. A wardrobe stylist provided me with two outfits to wear to auditions and said I would need to get a new pair of shoes. How was I going to do that? I began to panic. Maybe the wardrobe stylist thought I had parents who loved me. I remembered that the dime store carried shoes. I asked if it would be okay to wear plain white tennis shoes.

I hated girls who wore plain white tennis shoes, and now I was going to be one of them. I don't play tennis, but I'd slept on the tennis courts. I thought about the nights I would lie on the cold concrete and run my hands over it. I would imagine the shoes on the feet of those who laughed and played there during the day— crisp, clean, plain white tennis shoes. My stomach ached, and I felt sick. The stylist asked for my shoe size and promised to try to send the agency a pair of shoes. I began to panic again, because now I would need to have Johnny drive me back to Los Angeles to pick them up. Why was everything always so difficult?

I received a phone call at Johnny's parents' home. A modeling agency from Tokyo was coming to Los Angeles and wanted to meet with me. I could not believe what I was hearing—someone actually wanted me! I immediately pretended that the people from the agency were my parents, and they were flying here to take me home. I had no idea of how far Tokyo was from Los Angeles, but I did not care. I just wanted to go home to a place where someone was glad I was there. I walked into the agency in my best body-conscious dress and those ugly white tennis shoes. The "bookers"— the agency representatives who connect the models with the clients in the fashion industry—commented on my choice of outfit and asked why I hadn't worn the clothes they provided for me. I tried to explain that I felt beautiful in my skin-tight orange micro-mini dress and wanted the people from Tokyo to notice me. My bookers explained that all modeling agencies, including the one that was visiting from Tokyo, want to represent girls who are young and fresh, not overtly sexual. I didn't know what that meant, but I remember thinking, *This is my one chance at getting a real home in a faraway land, and I am not gonna let you blow it. I am already in your ugly white tennis shoes. Leave me alone.*

There were about thirty other girls at the audition. We each signed in and sized each other up. We were all "new faces" and eager to make it in the fashion world. The competitive energy in the room was palpable. I began to feel nauseated. As I walked to the bathroom, I passed the conference room with the clients. The Tokyo representatives noticed me right away, smiled, and asked me to come in. The owners of the Los Angeles agency sat beside the Tokyo bookers. Another model was patiently standing in front of them as they flipped through her book as if they were shuffling a deck of cards. She was beautiful, poised, soft-spoken, and totally different from me.

I entered the room and stood beside her. All of the attention was now on me. Was it my dress? Did I look homeless? Did they know about the beatings? Were my bruises showing? They closed the other model's book without even looking at all of the pages and began to ask me questions. She stood beside me with her head bowed and became invisible. This amazingly beautiful girl was now jealous of this homeless one. Everything in my being wanted to console her and whisper, "I am an illusion, and you are the lucky one."

Getting a passport was challenging. I begged my mother to

sign the documents to allow me to get a passport and move to Tokyo, but she refused. My mom was convinced that I would be traded into a sex-slave organization. She did not believe that the fashion industry would want me as a legitimate model. "You look like a boy. You have no tits, really short hair, and you are too fuckin' skinny. Who do you think you are, bitch? Twiggy?"

I needed my passport and had to find my dad, now more than ever, but I did not know where to start. I sat on a bench at a bus stop and concentrated. I tried to remember everything I could about my father—his girlfriends, the bars he frequented, the strip clubs he visited, his jobs, and the motels he lived in. I started down the line and refused to stop until I found him.

I located his family in another state and shared my fabulous news. I told them I was going to be fashion model and needed my dad's signature. I assured them that I did not need any money or want anything from my father, other than his signature on a piece of paper, allowing me to take this incredible job. Without any hesitation, my father signed the necessary forms, and I received my passport two weeks later.

My local agency gave me a list of things I would need to bring to Japan. As I read the list, I began to cry. I worked in retail during the day, but Johnny took all of my money. I borrowed a suitcase from his mother, filled it with packages of Ramen noodles and some clothes from the thrift store, and left for the airport. When I arrived at LAX, my mother was there. She was in her typical attire. Her five-foot-one, two-hundred-pound frame was adorned in a neon pink-and-green striped T-shirt. Her hair was a freshly colored orange from a supermarket box—she called it blonde. My mother had a megaphone and was screaming my name. I was horribly embarrassed by her outrageous behavior. I pretended I did not see her and tried to lose myself in the crowd. Panic overwhelmed me. I worried that someone from the modeling agency might see her and cancel my contract.

As I finally boarded the plane, I realized that I had escaped. As I took my seat, I looked around at all of the people. They were all smiling, and I tried to smile too. This was my first time on an airplane, and I was nervous and alone. A Disneyland ice skating team was on the same twelve-hour flight. As I eavesdropped on their conversations, I tried to soothe myself by feeling their joy. I imagined my new apartment and life ahead of me. As the plane took off, I began to cry. I was terrified to fly but petrified to stay. A flight attendant pushed a metal cart up and down the aisle, passing out hot washcloths. We were experiencing turbulence, and I was scared. I was holding onto the complimentary blanket and quickly reached to take the washcloth from her tongs. I looked around at the other passengers, because I did not know what I was supposed to do with it. I saw them put the washcloth over their faces and thought that meant we were going to crash. I started to cry out, "Oh, my God!"

The team of ice skaters explained we were fine. "The warm washcloth is to wash your face before the meal," one explained. I said, "I'm sorry. This is my first airplane ride." I thanked them for their reassurance.

My apartment was off the Hibiya Line—a subway line in Tokyo—and overlooked a cemetery. The building was filled with both male and females models from America, Brazil, New Zealand, and South Africa. I shared my room with a twelve-year-old model from Canada. She arrived with her parents and was so polite. Her mother stayed in our apartment for about a week and then flew home. It was nice having a mother there to talk to; I wished she could have stayed the entire two months.

Roppongi, the Tokyo district where my apartment was located, was the happening place. Its nightclubs offered a new experience. Agency models were put on the guest lists and given free drink tickets, so my twelve-year-old roommate and I went out almost every night. Food was always available, and the atmosphere was fast. American music played in the background, and the clubs were packed with foreign high-fashion models. I would spend the day on auditions, dreaming about the clubs I would attend that night. I loved to dance, and I needed food. The nightclubs were a godsend. I was so happy to know where my next meal was coming from and that I actually would be able to eat. Consistent bookings are hard to come by in the fashion world; there are so many beautiful models, all trying out for the same single spot. When I did land a campaign, a catalog, or an editorial, the international agency took 50 percent of each paycheck. Out of the 50 percent I got to keep, I had to repay my advances—money spent on airfare, apartment, test pictures, and related expenses. I was given a weekly allowance as an advance and spent most of it on postage. I would write letters to Johnny and creatively color on the envelopes to display my love. I was finally away from his beatings but found myself missing him. I wished I had a family to whom I could write letters, but all I had was Johnny.

He promised he would call me once a week, and he kept his promise. Our first phone call, however, did not go so well. When the phone rang, I answered "Muchi muchi," which is Japanese for hello. Johnny was furious and thought I was talking to someone else or saying a man's name. He told me he was going to beat me when I came home and I would never take another trip without him. I began to cry. Johnny must have really cared about me, because I made him mad enough to want to beat me and could no longer travel without him. Somehow, I felt relieved by his threats and comforted by knowing that I was in trouble.

After a long, hot summer day of auditions, I could not wait to escape to the clubs, into the land of dance. Somehow, when I was on the dance floor, I felt equal to the others. I was not my history. I was not my experiences. I was just a teenager, living in the moment. I wished I could dance forever. American music was very popular in the Tokyo club scene. Madonna's "Vogue" brought out the fashion model in the locals who were connected enough to make it into the elite establishment. Everyone was smiling; they seemed to be in a perfect state of bliss as we all posed to the beat on the dance floor.

Two beautiful male models from my agency were standing beside me at the bar. One was from Australia, and the other was from New York. We talked about high school, work, campaigns, jobs we had on hold, and the countries we called home. I felt important and beautiful. A few of my girlfriends had to leave the club, because they had to be on the set early the next morning. They asked me if I wanted to leave with them. The boys answered for me: "No." They promised to accompany me on the train and to my residence. I was ecstatic that such delicious male supermodels wanted to protect me. I didn't know that I actually would need protection from the two of them. I stayed at the bar and drank until I could barely stand. I was dripping with sweat and exhausted from dancing. That rare time had come when I actually wanted to leave. My balance was off, and I needed to lie down. With an arm over each of their shoulders, I walked out with them. Their models residence was walking distance, around the corner from the Roppongi clubs. They told me I was going to sleep there and then take the train home in the morning. I smiled and trusted them like the family I never had. I willfully went into their apartment. The door closed … and my life changed forever. There were several male models standing in the living room. I didn't recognize most of them, because they were with other agencies.

The model from Australia put me on the couch and started making out with me. The next thing I knew, another male model picked me up and carried me to the floor. I remember looking at the guy I was kissing and reaching for him. I was held down, and a needle went into my arm. I had never shot dope before and wondered what they were putting in me. My body felt heavy, and I could not move. My clothes were ripped off, and I lost consciousness. I woke up with a man inside me and my arms bound above my head with belts. I began to cry, and one of them snarled, "Shut up, bitch," which made me cry harder. One male model from my agency said, "Don't call her bitch; that's not cool."

I tried to move my head to see if I could get eye contact with anyone to help me. I was given another shot and passed out for several hours. When I came to, I was being raped with a sake bottle. I tried to fight. I kicked and screamed, but it was in slow motion. I continued to drift in and out of consciousness. There were five or six models standing over me the next time I woke up, and another one walked through the front door. I knew this one! He was with my agency and from California too. Maybe he would rescue me. He shook his head and said, "Dude, what the hell are you doing? She's still in high school." The other models did not stop and asked if he wanted a turn. He said "What the hell is wrong with you guys?" and walked out. How could he leave me there? Was he going to get help? Was he calling the agency? Was I going to be in trouble for staying out too late at the club? I wished I had left with the girls and not stayed to dance. I lost consciousness again, and when I woke up this time, I was in a bed with one of them. All of the other models had left. I was bleeding and in a lot of pain. I started crying and tried to stand, but I fell to my knees. The male model woke up and asked me to sit on the bed. I obeyed. He said, "Come here." And I did. He put himself inside me while I cried, begging him to hurry up and finish because it hurt. When he was done, I gathered my torn shorts from the floor. I held them on like a diaper to catch the blood, and I put on my one shoe. I asked if I could borrow some clothes to take the train home, but he said no and laughed at me.

I walked to the subway station and got on the train. I was a mess. I was beaten, bruised, and bleeding; my spirit died that day. The businesspeople on the train stared wide-eyed at this blonde foreign girl. I felt like an alien; I felt disgusting. Their condemnation pierced what was left of my soul. The daggers from their eyes were so cold, and I could not escape them. I endured the disdain and pictured my apartment. I kept telling myself, "You are almost there, you are almost there, you are almost there."

When I got to my apartment, the girls were already on the set. I closed the door and then collapsed on the floor behind it. I released the grip of the fabric that held my clothes on my body. The bloody shorts fell to the floor. I kicked off my one shoe and limped to the shower, where I tried to scrub off the dirt. It did not matter how much I tried to clean myself; I could not wash away the filth. The blood would not stop. I had to go to the hospital.

I called another model and asked her to come over. She was nineteen and knew the two guys who were supposed to take care of me the night before. She began to cry when saw me. She put me in a taxi, and off to the hospital we went. The doctors notified the agency of my condition. After I recovered from the attacks, I was sent back to the States. I lost my international contract. I lost my apartment. I lost my chance to be somebody. I lost my spirit. How was I going to explain coming home early to Johnny?

Johnny met me at the airport without flowers, without a gift, and without a hug. I had imagined him holding balloons, a handmade sign, and twirling me around with gentle kisses. He just stood there, staring at me. I wondered if he could sense my deception and feel my betrayal from across the seas. I suppose I did not deserve a welcome-home celebration. As I enviously looked at the families rejoicing with their loved ones coming off the plane, my heart ached, and I tried not to cry. I wanted to know love more than I wanted to breathe. Johnny immediately accused me of sleeping with another guy on my trip. I denied it, but my eyes said something else. I could not help but have a smirk on my face. Knowing that I was desired by other men made me feel powerful. He stared at me, tilted his head, and then swiftly walked toward another terminal without speaking. I didn't know where he was going, but I followed him anyway. He was mad, but he would not hit me in public. I knew I was going to get a beating as soon as we got home, and oddly, I was relieved to know he still cared.

In between punches, I tried to explain that what had happened with the guys from the club. Johnny continued to hit me and scream, "I forbid you from talking to guys, whore. What the fuck made you think you had permission to go to a club?" Since I had disobeyed him, Johnny beat me until I passed out. The next morning, he told me how much gas money I owed him for picking me up from the airport, and he threatened to slice my face if I ever disobeyed him again.

Does anyone ever look past a model's appearance and search for a higher meaning, which her soul screams out in the silence of a picture?

Adventures in Abuse

I landed another modeling contract, this one in Taipei, Taiwan. Taipei was the land of the free, and I was in need of some serious freedom. I promised Johnny that if he allowed me to go, I would not go out to clubs or talk to boys for the entire two months I was in Taiwan. He finally agreed but under one condition: he was going to fly there to check up on me. I had mixed feelings about Johnny flying to Taipei, but at least I had some breathing room until he arrived.

My apartment was directly across the hall from the agency. It was a three-bedroom unit, and I had it all to myself until my roommate arrived. This agency was much smaller than the one I was with in Tokyo. In Japan, male and female models were housed separately. Here, there were together. Soon after I arrived, a male model (I'll call him Aiden) arrived from Australia and joined me in my humble abode. He was in his late twenties and beautiful. He loved James Bond movies ... and men. I felt safe with Aiden, except when he would bring home strange guys and have sex with them in our living room. I could hear everything. The sexual sounds reopened deep childhood wounds that lay hidden in my soul. I remembered that as a little girl, I put a pillow over each ear, folding my earlobes up and squeezing as tightly as I could with my forearms, to drown out the sounds that scared me.

While living with Aiden, I was terrified when I needed to use the bathroom in the middle of the night and would have to open my bedroom door to get to our only bathroom. At age seventeen, I found myself crying into my pillow and begging God to take away my urge to void until sunrise. My prayers were not always answered, and sometimes I opened the door and just pretended I didn't see them having intercourse.

Nevertheless, Aiden was genuinely kind and funny, and when he was not having sex with men in front of me, he made me smile a lot. I worried about Johnny's upcoming visit and his imagining I'd been unfaithful to him with my beautiful roommate. I tried to stay focused and concentrate on work, but fear began to engulf my spirit as the days grew closer to his arrival. And each evening brought its own terror because of Aiden and his lovers.

Meanwhile, I met Lucas, and he was my escape. He was a lovely Brazilian male model with my agency, and we began to date. He lived in a different models residence, but I wished he lived in mine. One night after dinner, Lucas took me to a tiny club that played American music. The deejay repeatedly played "Sweet Child o' Mine" by Guns N' Roses. Although Lucas's native language was Portuguese, he sang to me in English. "She's got eyes of the bluest skies, as if they thought of rain; I'd hate to look into those eyes and see an ounce of pain." I wondered if he could sense my journey or feel my brokenness. As the music played, Lucas sang, and time stood still. Unfortunately, Johnny was coming to Taipei the following morning. I knew that I would never be able to see Lucas again, unless I flew to Brazil, so it seemed pointless to open up to him emotionally and become even more attached to him. I wanted to be with Lucas more than I wanted to breathe. I liked how I felt beside him. He made me feel important. He never hurt me.

The next morning I took a taxi to the international airport and anxiously awaited Johnny's arrival. I was nervous, excited, scared, and disappointed all at the same time. I could not stop thinking about Lucas. While I waited for Johnny's plane to land,

I called Lucas from a pay phone. Hearing his voice centered me, and all of my worldly concerns vanished. Lucas begged to see me again that evening. I tried to explain that a "friend" from the States was coming to visit, and I had to entertain my guest. Lucas insisted we all meet up for dinner. I loved that idea. I knew how risky it was, but I agreed anyway. Regardless of the consequences that lay ahead, I had to be with Lucas one last time. My body, my mind, my soul, and my spirit desired him.

I sat down on a cold plastic chair and waited for Johnny. Eventually, through a sea of people, Johnny became visible. He was holding his acoustic guitar in one hand, and dragging his luggage in the other. He smiled as he walked toward me. I stood there, praying for the strength to smile back at him. I hugged him, and we walked out of the terminal together. He commented on my outfit, saying I looked like a tramp, even though I was dressed conservatively. I realized just how quickly my life had changed back to what I'd run away from. I apologized to Johnny for upsetting him with my outfit. I handed a taxi driver a piece of paper with my address written in Chinese, and we got in the cab. The ride back to my residence was awkward. I tried to lighten the mood by telling Johnny I had a special night planned, and we were going out to a traditional dinner that evening. I was worried he might say he was too tired after the long flight, but he agreed. Johnny seemed impressed with himself. He grabbed me around my neck with his forearm and pulled me in close, saying, "I knew you loved me. All those beatings must have knocked some sense into you. You better not fuck up this trip."

Our driver looked into his rearview mirror to check on my reaction to Johnny's condescending and rude comments. I smiled and nodded as if to signal that I was okay, and our driver looked away. I assumed that all taxi drivers in Taipei did not speak English, but perhaps I was wrong.

The restaurant was dark, smoky, and very crowded. We walked in and headed toward the back of the room. I hadn't told Johnny that we were meeting Lucas. I was hoping we could just walk by his table, and he would ask us to join him, and that is exactly what happened. Lucas stood up to greet us. He shook hands with Johnny and smiled at me. I think Lucas knew that Johnny was more than just a "friend"—he was very discreet with his affection toward me. When Johnny was looking at the menu, Lucas smiled and winked at me. I had butterflies in my tummy and was genuinely happy. I'd never felt like this before.

Somehow, Johnny sensed my joy, and it infuriated him. He leaned over to me and whispered, "Bitch, I fuckin' told you not to talk to guys. Wait until we get home." I knew what that meant, but I didn't even care. Johnny was on my schedule now. He was in a foreign country and had no idea how to get back to my residence without me. He had to wait until Lucas and I were finished with our meals, and we took our time eating, laughing, and staring into each other's eyes. It was as if we were the only two people in that crowded restaurant, and our time together was the only thing that mattered. I tried to memorize each and every moment in order to make it last forever. That way, when Johnny was beating me, I could travel to this marvelous place in my mind and be present with Lucas in spirit.

Aiden was not home when Johnny and I returned to my residence. All of the lights were off, and it was dark. I panicked, because without Aiden, my beating was going to be worse. Johnny slammed the front door shut and punched me in the neck. I fell to the living room floor. I had a photo shoot the next morning, so I curled up in fetal position and tried to protect my face. I wondered how the makeup artist was going to hide swollen bruises. The agency was located right next door, and I worried that someone might be there later than usual and would hear him beating me. If they canceled my contract, then where would I live? Johnny kicked me in my back. He became more enraged and started calling me names. He demanded I turn on the lights, so he could see the piece of shit he was beating some sense into, and I obeyed. Johnny grabbed my hair and pulled me into the nearest bedroom, which was Aiden's. I was really in trouble now. I tried to grasp a vision of Lucas and concentrate on his smile to take away some of the pain. I had to leave my body and mentally travel to another place, or I would not survive. I could hear guys' voices coming from the kitchen—Aiden was home! Johnny slammed me into the wall and called me a whore for living with guys. I grabbed Aiden's dresser and tried to hold on while Johnny dragged me to the bed. The dresser crashed down on the wood floor. I screamed for Aiden, but he never came to help me. Johnny suffocated me with pillows because I was screaming and fighting back. I woke up the next morning on the floor—bloody, embarrassed, and humiliated, with Johnny's urine in my hair.

Two weeks passed, and it was finally time for Johnny to fly home. I was so happy when it was time for him to leave. It had been difficult to focus on work with the constant fear of retaliation for working with male models. I was a fashion model. I did not book the talent; I *was* the talent. Johnny never understood that concept. He beat me anyway. Sometimes, my shoots would be with me alone, but other times they would include a group. I never knew if I was the only model booked on the job until I arrived on the set. Johnny always grilled me about who would be on the set, and I always lied. Anxiety was my middle name; I was in a constant state of panic. I tried to mask my fears with laughter, numb my sorrows with alcohol, and cure my pain with drugs. As a cover girl, everything I ever needed to take away my pain was free. I began to love my toxic candy—I could never get enough.

The agency never mentioned hearing my screams from Johnny's distraction. I was surprised that Aiden didn't tell my secret, but perhaps he was guilty of looking in the other direction and felt too much shame for ignoring my cries for help. Aiden and I never spoke of that night or of the nights I saw him having sex with men in our living room. Aiden and I lived in a land of unspoken agreement. I wanted out. I thought, *How much longer until my two months are up?*

Ciao Bella

$\mathcal{M}$y plane landed in Milan, Italy. I gathered my luggage and approached the exit. As I walked off the plane, I saw a lovely man in a suit, holding a sign with my name on it. He was my driver. I walked toward him, feeling loved. Although it was his job to bring me to my residence, his handwritten sign, smile, and warm greeting was something I had waited for my entire life. I enjoyed the drive into the city and knew that this trip was going to be different. I wanted to go to my apartment and take a shower after my long flight, but I was told that I must weigh in at the agency before he could drive me to my residence. Panic set in. I was wearing my glasses, jeans, and a T-shirt. I wasn't dressed for an audition. I started to worry. If they saw me like this, would they send me home? I asked the driver to pull over so I could get something out of my suitcase, and he graciously complied with my request. I pulled out my makeup bag and quickly applied lip gloss, perfume, and mascara. I put in my contacts and fixed my hair. I wanted to change my outfit too. My driver told me not to worry about my clothes; he said as soon I got to the agency, they would to ask me to take them off anyway. I was comforted yet oddly concerned at the same time.

As we were on our way to the agency, he told me that he'd been the main agency driver for the last fifteen years. He then explained what I should expect when we arrived. "You'll be put in a bathroom with your main booker. You'll be wearing only panties, and you'll be measured and weighed. The numbers will then be compared to the measurements in your contract." If a model's weight was more than 4.8 pounds over the weight listed in her contract, the agency would cancel her contract and immediately drive her back to the airport to send her home. My driver assured me that I would be fine and told me not to worry. He was right. I measured five-foot-nine and 103.6 pounds. Perfection.

The agency said I was going to do very well in Milan, and they treated me like a princess from the moment I arrived. I did not have to live in a typical models residence. I lived in a palace, with one other female model from Brazil and an Italian police officer. My bedroom was huge, with blonde wood floors and French doors that opened up to my personal veranda. It was the most incredible place I ever called home, and I felt safe there. I loved Italy, and Italy loved me. I shot two magazine covers my first week there. In my second week, I had the honor of flying to Spain to shoot an amazing editorial for a popular Italian magazine. I loved Milan. It was romantic and beautiful, and even the grandmas who rode the tram were dressed to perfection.

Milan had breathtaking buildings and incredible churches. On Sunday mornings, I would go to mass inside the Duomo—the Milan Cathedral—and felt like I was in heaven. I wished I could live there forever, but nobody would want me for that long. I knew that everything came to an end and soon, this blessing would be a distant memory too. I tried to stay present, in the moment, and embrace all the city had to offer without worrying about where I would live next. Somehow, that always seemed to work itself out.

I booked another cover that was shooting in Poland. I flew there in a private plane and could not believe how amazing my life was actually turning out to be. The client picked me up at the airport and drove me to his home. I thought it was very odd that he personally picked me up instead of sending a driver. He told me that all of the models from Milan stayed at his home because it was very spacious, and that is where I would be staying too. I wondered why the agency did not mention that I would be lodging at his personal residence. As soon as I got in his car, he instructed me to give him my passport so he could put it in the safe when we arrived.

"I've never had a client request to hold my passport before," I said.

"Every girl with your agency has allowed me to hold her passport," he assured me. "It's a standard precaution in Poland. I'm just complying with a request made from your agency in Italy."

I reluctantly handed him my passport, but I couldn't ignore the uneasy feeling I had in my stomach. I started to pay attention to route he drove from the airport to his residence, but I couldn't read the street signs. I couldn't memorize buildings, because all I saw were bare trees and gray sky. I did see what I thought were bus benches, and I counted them as we drove past, trying to get a type of orientation.

We finally arrived at our destination. It was modest, not even close to the grandeur of my palace in Italy. Everything inside my being was telling me something was not right. He showed me to my room. It had two doors, a traditional one with an inside lock that connected to the kitchen and another one that folded accordion-style and slid open loudly. He told me dinner would be served shortly, and he would call me when it was ready.

He made pasta and poured me a glass of red wine. I thanked him, but then lied, saying I didn't drink alcohol. After dinner, I wanted to take a shower and go to sleep. I had a 5:00 a.m. call time and really wanted to be well rested for my cover. The more covers a model shoots in Europe, the more money she can make back in the States. Since I was there to build my book, I needed to make every photo shoot count. I locked the door before I went to bed … and awoke in the middle of the night with the client nibbling on my ear. I was startled but could not move.

I asked what he was doing, and he said that he had an arrangement with my agency in Italy that every girl he booked for a cover would sleep with him. I refused; I said I had a boyfriend and would never be unfaithful. He tried to persuade me by telling me the names of other models who shot covers with him and kept the agency agreement. I graciously declined again. "I will understand if you don't want me to shoot your cover," I said. "I'll be fine with your sending me back to Milan early."

He seemed taken aback by my assertiveness and embarrassed by my refusal to sleep with him. He was not forceful or loud; he was just disappointed. As he left the room, he said only, "Get a good night's rest. I'll see you in the morning." As soon as he left, I locked my bedroom door again, although I wasn't sure what good it would do—he'd already unlocked it once. Still, I felt a little bit safer in doing so. It was impossible for me to get back to sleep. I couldn't stop wondering if he was going to come back into my room and rape me. I started to cry and pray to God that I would make it back to Milan safely.

Morning finally came. I was extremely grateful that he never came back into my room that night. I thanked him for allowing me to get some rest, even though I had not slept a wink. He still had my passport, which made me very nervous. As we drove to the studio, I tried to read the Polish road signs, but they were confusing. I started to cry. I was very scared that he was going hurt me since I refused to sleep with him.

"Don't worry," he said. "And please don't mention last night to anyone." When I agreed, he offered to put me up in a hotel for the final night. I was so relived! We shot the cover and a several-page editorial. The Polaroids used to test the lighting looked amazing. I just wanted the client to be happy, return my passport, and have his pilot fly me back to Italy. And that is exactly what he did the next day. When I was finally back in Milan, I went to the agency, where I took my booker aside and told her what had happened in Poland. She attempted to comfort me but then starting speaking rapidly in Italian to the other bookers.

I could feel the energy shift in the room, and then she became angry with me. "Sometimes a model has to overlook certain things," she said tersely, "and if you want to be a good model, you will do the same." I was confused. I felt like I'd let them down and worried that since I'd made them angry, they would send me home. I loved Milan and never wanted to leave. I regretted mentioning any of it to the agency.

I booked another job, this time shooting with the house photographer for one of the biggest fashion magazines in Europe. Having the opportunity to work with such greatness could propel a new face into the land of supermodel glory. It was every model's dream to shoot with him, and he wanted to shoot with me!

The agency told me that this photographer liked to masturbate when he took pictures of their girls but that I should try to ignore it. Some of the girls on the covers he shot looked very young, like me, but others were in their midtwenties and household names. I wondered if each of them really experienced what I was being prepared to walk into. The agency suggested I drink a bottle of wine before I went to the set.

I really did not want to take this job, but I was too afraid of being sent home if I refused. I knew that the wrath of Johnny would be worse than anything I would experience with this photographer. I considered the caliber of girls he worked with and remembered the agency's reaction to my experience in Poland. I smiled and agreed to shoot the cover with this incredibly famous photographer. I took my booker's advice and arrived on the set a little tipsy. He offered me a glass of wine, and I graciously accepted. I sat in hair and makeup, getting totally drunk.

He soon closed the set and asked everyone to leave. I changed into my wardrobe and was relieved to see that I was shooting in long pants and long sleeves. As I walked onto the closed set, my body began to shake. The photographer asked me if I was cold. I was not cold; I was scared. As he shot pictures of me, he slowly began to expose himself, just as the agency said he would. The lights on the set were extremely bright, but I could see the shape of another adult in the distance. The photographer came closer to me and put his camera down. He told me to sit on his lap. I obeyed. I did not want that other person in the distance coming over to hurt me too. The photographer licked my neck and bounced me on his knee. I allowed him to touch me. I tried to tell myself that he would be finished soon and that the agency would be proud of me for not resisting him. I escaped into the land of imagination, where I visualized myself on the cover of another magazine, living in a place where I was finally free of men who desired me.

Birth of Change

I returned to Taipei after landing another two-month contract with a different agency in China. I was so grateful to have a place to call home for two more months. Most agencies had traditional models residences. I was assured that I would be given my own room without any male model roommates, and that was good enough for me. When I arrived in Taipei this time, I was put up in a hotel-style apartment building. The entire complex was filled with models from two different agencies. International male models were housed on separate floors from the female models. There was a twenty-four-hour desk clerk in the lobby.

I was handed my room key when I arrived and instructed to return it to the front desk when I went out on auditions. Although the desk clerk did not speak English, I felt safer, knowing he would always be downstairs if I needed him. I promised myself that I would not make any friends or trust anyone on this trip. I decided to focus on fashion and writing poetry, instead of going out to the clubs. At exactly 11:30 p.m. on March 16, 1993, I felt moved to write the words "faith so strong it burns inside, brightly lighting the way." In the middle of writing this poem, the entire apartment complex had a blackout. I scribbled the last part of the poem, "brightly lighting the way," on my paper in the dark as I sat on my bed and then waited until the lights returned.

Several models were in the halls, laughing and being childish. I was too intrigued with the universe's timing of the blackout to join in their festivities. The electricity returned in about five minutes. I sat there staring at my poem and feeling very connected to God. I needed to speak with someone about what just had happened, but who would understand this? I decided to go to my neighbor's apartment. She was an older model, about twenty-three, and seemed very wise; as she did not frequent the clubs or drink alcohol. I shared my experience with her, and she said, "I'm not surprised." She smiled, and her eyes beamed with light and love. I felt as though she was looking right through me. Her voice was reassuring and calm, but how could she not be surprised with such a supernatural event? Did such things happen to her frequently? Did they happen to all of us, but we were too preoccupied to notice? Her comment made me a little afraid, and I could not stop questioning her unshakeable serenity during such an extraordinary time. I thought this was a totally odd experience, but it did not seem to faze her at all.

This apartment had a television, and I was so excited to watch TV, even if I couldn't understand a word of it. The desk clerk had a video player that connected to every television in the building. Any movie that he put in the VCR at the front desk was displayed for all to see, and this was how my life really began to change. Someone had given the desk clerk a DVD of a lecture by Louise Hay called *You Can Heal Your Life*. The clerk ran that lecture over and over again. She spoke English, so regardless of the topic, I was hooked. Her voice was kind and gentle. I could feel the compassion spring forth from her soul and hug my broken heart. I wondered what my life would have been like if I had been born into her family instead of mine. I felt safe when that DVD was on. I began to think about different perspectives when I listened to Louise Hay speak. I felt important and valuable, and those were new feelings for me. I remember her as a beautiful grandmother with short hair, wearing a white sweater, and standing on a huge stage as she shared her wisdom with those in her class. She walked back and forth, telling very long stories. Because of the age of the students that sat in front of her, I figured she was a college professor, and I really wanted to know at which school she taught. If that was what college was like, I wanted to go there too.

When I arrived back in the States, I began auditioning for television commercials too. Although I was not in the Screen Actors Guild, the agency sent me on an audition for a union commercial on PBS. And … I booked the job. The director was aware that I was not in the union but loved me and arranged it with SAG so that I could shoot the commercial. It also allowed me to get my foot halfway in the SAG door. I was so excited to have the opportunity to be eligible to obtain my SAG card. I prayed that I would land another union spot really soon. I was moving up in the world, and people were graciously blessing me with enormous compassion. I felt like a real actor, a real somebody, and I liked it.

Life with Johnny, however, was the same. He beat me if I booked a job, and he beat me if didn't. He drove me to my auditions in the Mercedes I paid for and watched me like a hawk as I walked inside the casting locations. If boys with my agency so much as even said hello to me in front of Johnny, fear would engulf my belly, because I knew what would happen when we got home.

I knew a lot of male models. We all circulated within the same countries, saw each other on castings, and partied in the same clubs. Some of them picked up on my distant behavior when we were in the States. I was afraid that people knew why I was scared. Johnny said he beat me because I was stupid. Were the models starting to figure out that I was stupid too? Were they going to beat me next? Would the agency drop me if they found out I was stupid?

Johnny drove me to a national commercial casting and waited in the car, as usual. I felt sad and empty inside, but I tried to hide it as I signed in and waited my turn. I looked around at all of the other girls, and they were so beautiful. What was I even doing here? Why did they request to see me? I went to the restroom, looked in the mirror, and cried. I knew that I needed to book this job to get my SAG card, but I thought, *If I was the casting director, I would totally hire someone else.*

I'd heard someone come in while I was in the stall, so I put on my best fake smile and pretend bubbly personality as I exited the stall. Two girls were standing in front of the mirror, applying lipstick and reading a script with each other. I smiled at them, wondering if they too had a "Johnny" waiting in the car.

I signed in, and the assistant took my Polaroids, stapled them to a white piece of paper, and handed it back to me. I sat by myself, listening to others laughing and wondering if it was real. I never laughed like that. How could they be so carefree? I could act like I was the happiest girl in the world, and everyone believed it, but inside, I was dying. I reached into my bag and grabbed my compact. I felt my nose start to tingle, and I knew that the tears would quickly follow. I needed to make sure that no one saw tears fall down my cheeks. I told myself, "You got this," and closed my compact, just as I heard my name called.

I stood up and put on my best "I am on top of the world, and everything is fabulous" show, and I entered the studio. There was a panel of people inside the room, and they seemed to love me. They enjoyed my enthusiasm, laughed at my jokes, complimented my looks, and said I had the most darling personality. I left the audition feeling good about myself, but as I left the building and walked toward the car, it all faded away.

The following week, I received the news—I got the job! My agent seemed more excited than I was about it, but it was a big deal—it was a union commercial; I was now a member of the Screen Actors Guild. Union jobs paid way more than nonunion jobs. I decided not to tell Johnny about the news; I focused on planning my escape. He could have the car, my apartment, the furniture— everything. I just needed to close my credit card accounts and keep my portfolio with me at all times. I knew he would destroy it if he knew what I was planning to do. Johnny always told me he would slice my face so I would not be able to work, but I was more worried about him possibly destroying pictures.

I began to take inventory of my things. I canceled all of the credit cards and opened a new account without him as an authorized user. I was at work when Johnny went to Guitar Center, and his credit card was declined. I had no idea what I was about to walk into when I got home. I opened the door, and a volcano erupted right in front of me. He began to swing at my face, and I ducked. He grabbed me by the neck and threw me on the bed. He punched, kicked, and strangled me until I passed out. When I woke up, he was in the living room, watching TV. I grabbed the phone and dialed the number of a girlfriend—I'll call her Angel—who was with my agency. I didn't speak to her but placed the phone beside the desk. I knew that she would be able to hear if he killed me. When Johnny noticed I was up, the beatings began again. I screamed, but no one came. I begged and pleaded for him to stop, but he did not.

The next morning he went out for coffee, and I grabbed the phone. Angel had stayed up all night, listening to my cries and waiting for me to speak to her. When she heard my voice, she began to cry herself. "You are leaving today," she told me. "I will be at your apartment to pick you up." Johnny always went to band practice at the same time, so I knew when he would be out. I still was terrified that he would return while Angel and I were packing our cars, but I knew she right; I needed to go. It was now or never.

The coast was clear—or was it? Angel came over, and we quickly threw my things into both cars. We piled them up so high that neither of us could see out of our back windows. I put my teddy bear named Dreamer in the front seat next to me, and we drove to her mother's home. I was sobbing and full of regret. *Johnny loves me!* I thought. *What am I doing?* The farther we drove from my apartment, the more desperation I felt. I was crying hysterically, and I could feel the stares of the other drivers as I waited at red lights. I was homeless. Again.

I decided I was going to move to New York, get an apartment, and start over. I just had to finish my last few bookings in California, and then I would be on my way. This was the last job I was scheduled to shoot, and then I would fly out the next morning. I went to the studio and shot a campaign. The photographer, makeup artist, wardrobe stylist, and client never had any idea of what was going on behind my infectious smile. I am a magician, and I made myself turn into anything they wanted. I knew how to pretend; I'd been doing that my whole life.

When I finished work, Johnny was waiting outside for me. I was not afraid. I was happy to see him. He apologized for his actions and asked me to come home. He told me that his father had been diagnosed with cancer and that was why the last beating been worse than all of the others. Something about that sounded wrong to me, and I began to feel brief periods of disgust rise up from my soul. I told him I needed to leave, but then asked him how he knew where I was shooting.

Johnny just smiled and softly said, "Bitch, I know everything." I turned to walk away, but he walked behind me. I walked faster, and he walked faster. I knew I was in real trouble, so I began to run. I ran around the corner and back into the studio. I told the photographer that my ex-boyfriend was outside, and I was afraid. Several guys went downstairs and tried to talk to Johnny, and while they distracted him, another moved my car. They told me to exit the back of the building while Johnny was preoccupied. I was so was embarrassed that I'd had to ask for help. All I kept thinking was, *Well, at least I'm moving to New York, and hopefully I will never see these people again.*

One of the production assistants hurried me into my car, and I sped away. Unfortunately, I turned the wrong way, and when I made a U-turn, Johnny saw me! He jumped in the Mercedes and chased me. I drove dangerously, in and out of traffic, until I lost him. How did he know where to find me? Where would he be next? I was too afraid to stop driving but more afraid that I would see him on the road beside me. I circled the city and surrounding cites until it got dark. I figured it would be next to impossible for him to follow me at night. When I got back to Angel's place, I collapsed on the bed in tears. Her mother knocked on the bedroom door, asking if I was all right. I minimized it … I lied. I thought if she knew how upset I really was, she would not want me there … and then where would I go? I didn't want to be alone, so I wiped my tears, painted on a smile, and joined her in the kitchen. She made me tea, and together we watched reruns of her favorite soap opera.

Junkyard Dog

I was living in New York, at the peak of my career in the fashion industry. I'd finally made it into American *Vogue* and landed an enormous perfume campaign, which plastered my image on billboards across the country. Life was finally perfect. I was independent. I was successful. I was unstoppable. I was in demand. And then … I met him.

Preston was everything I thought I wanted in a man. He was beautiful … and lost. He was a heroin addict, living inside a halfway house, and a convicted criminal. Preston had street credit, and although I was far removed from my homeless roots, somehow I took comfort in his status, and I periodically rested in his abusive presence. While we were dating, I was warned by his friends that he was "gnarly," but I foolishly disregarded their comments. Preston would share stories with me of shoving his previous girlfriend into a cardboard box and throwing her down a flight of stairs and of punching another one in the mouth when she asked him a question at the wrong time, but I never thought he would turn on me. I thought I could tame Preston and help him get off heroin by encouraging him to move out of the halfway house and move in with me. Preston just needed love, and if I could love him enough to make him stop shooting dope, maybe he could love me enough to make me feel safe.

Preston and I dated for about two months before he proposed to me. We were engaged to be married, and it was now time to meet his family. Preston knew that I was a runaway but still seemed confident that his family would approve of me. I always felt less than other people because I didn't have a family of my own. I imagined that Preston had come from a similar situation because he wrestled with such powerful demons, and he asked me not to look at him differently after he introduced me to his parents.

As we drove towards his parents' home, we passed a trailer park on the side of the road. I began to feel more comfortable and confident that Preston and I had a lot more in common than I originally thought. But then we kept driving ... and finally arrived at one of the most opulent gated communities I had ever seen. As a model, I had shot campaigns in some of the most luxurious locations in the world, but this surpassed any of them. His parents lived in a palace, protected by two-thousand–pound doors. There were twelfth-century fireplaces, solid gold walls, and ancient artifacts that they often loaned to museums for periodic display. The homes in this community belonged to the most elite of society and regularly graced the pages of prestigious architectural magazines. His family built hospitals, churches, religious schools, and museums. Private jets, butlers, elevators, and unlimited resources were the norm. His family was lovely and sophisticated, and they welcomed me with open arms.

I did not understand Preston's decision to leave such security for the uncertainty of thug life, nor could I ever imagine the pressure to excel that poor little boy experienced, having been born into such a coveted environment. Preston was a typical child, mischievous in nature and curious about the world. He was a creative and free-spirited little boy, full of wonder—and this created discord in the land of wealth and social privilege. Thus, he was sent away from the family.

He began experimenting with drugs at the tender age of ten and then was institutionalized for most of teenage years in various behavior modification and drug rehabilitation facilities. Unfortunately, his parents unwittingly sent him to an out-of-state treatment center that was later closed after it was found responsible for the abuse and deaths of several children. Beautiful Preston was the victim of abuse at the hands of those entrusted to care for him.

~

*P*reston did not like to be alone. I took him with me whenever possible to various locations when I was working. He attended most of my photo shoots—until he showed up drunk to a fashion show. I remember being backstage in hair and makeup and hearing everyone talk about "someone" getting into a fight and putting a cigarette out on an announcer's head, screaming, "Where's Hope? I want to see Hope! Where's my wife?"

I knew they were speaking about Preston. He was escorted out of the show to the curb, where the police were waiting for him. My stomach dropped, and I began to feel sick, but I had to take the stage anyway. I took a deep breath, entered on my cue, and walked the runway. As I walked to the beat of the music, my mind was going a million miles an hour. I knew that I could no longer take Preston with me to work, but I had no idea how I was going to tell him.

I felt so connected to Preston. He needed me to breathe, and I needed him to feel secure. I didn't want him to be sad and then shoot more dope to fix the pain. As I walked off the stage, I realized that my presence made Preston feel safe too. He was like my child, and at the time, I thought his neediness was sweet. It felt wonderful to be wanted by such a strong man.

Preston slowly changed my name to Bitch. Cunt. Fucking Retard. And I answered him when he called me. He only used my real name when we were out in public. He was charming and charismatic, and everyone liked him. I knew that when he called me Hope, he was cringing inside. Preston said I did not deserve to be called Hope, because I was a "thing," and I should have been aborted, but my mother was just too fuckin' stupid. I used to imagine that when he called me those names, he really meant babe, doll, honey. I made excuses for his vulgarity and justified his rage. Preston said he never hated anyone as much as he hated me, and that should tell me how much he loved me. And ... I understood him.

Mommy Make Him Stop!

*A*t age twenty-four, I was married and at risk for sudden death, but not at the hands of my husband. I had collapsed at a car wash and woke up in the emergency room. I was told that I had a congenital cardiac abnormality and needed emergency heart surgery, or I would die. I was not afraid of dying; I was actually relieved! I was afraid of living. I felt comforted by my poor prognosis. I saw it as a reward from the universe for having endured so much pain in my lifetime. It was like a hug from God, reassuring me that I was not alone and was close to coming home, to a place where I was finally wanted.

Although Preston's parents found me the best surgeon in the world, I died on the table on December 3, 1997. And when that legendary surgeon restarted my heart, I birthed an unfathomable endurance, having been reenergized from the hand of God himself and an unfathomable love for humanity.

All I ever wanted was to have a family of my own. After my heart healed and I received clearance from my cardiologist, Preston and I decided to start our family; we envisioned a Supermodel daughter, followed by a Rockstar son! Preston's parents hired a judge to seal his criminal record, and we went to a holistic healer for alternative purification. I wanted to make sure my mind, body, and spirit were entirely ready for conception. I was preoccupied with becoming pregnant and was given herbs to cleanse my body and prepare for motherhood. This holistic doctor was extremely intuitive. Even though I told him nothing about my childhood, he described several blocks in my chakras— the energy centers in the body. He reassured me that I could release my fears into a loving universe, as they stood in the way of my achieving my desires. After that, my baby would soon be on its way.

He encouraged me to relax and trust the process of life. He explained that at my point of surrender and true acceptance, the world would align me with purpose and grant my desires. There was a trick, though—I had to believe with my spirit and soul that I was worthy of love in order to realign my energy and balance my chi. He told me I was going to be a wonderful mother. His eyes hugged my brokenness, and I surrendered.

I vividly remember the night we conceived our daughter. As suggested by my holistic doctor, I kept my legs lifted high in the air in order to aid in Preston's female sperm a quicker path into my uterus. I visualized my tiny egg welcoming his seed and implantation taking place. I stayed in that position for over an hour, touching my belly and softly saying, "I love you, sweet girl," to the creation that would soon become our daughter. I believed, and I conceived!

The first time Preston hit me, I was holding our beautiful little baby girl. She was only three months old when his fist first met my skull. I held on tightly to our infant daughter as I fell over on the floor. I kept thinking, *Dear God, please don't let me drop her.* I remember it as if it were yesterday. Preston cussed me out, saying, "Look what you made me do, bitch. Why couldn't you of just shut the fuck up when I told you to?" He grabbed his keys, spit on my face, and walked out the front door, slamming it shut. I lay there on the floor, holding our baby girl and crying, wishing he hadn't left. I wondered what I'd done wrong. I had an intense headache and was getting terrible chest pain. I called his parents for help—I didn't know what else to do.

His father drove me to the emergency room while his mother watched our daughter. When the doctor asked me what happened, I lied. I did not want Preston to get into trouble. I was sure he hadn't meant to hurt me this bad, and I was sure he was sorry too. When I got out of the hospital, I asked Preston's mother if the baby and I could stay with them for a few days. His mother said no. She told me Preston was my problem now, and she didn't want him coming over to their home, strung out on drugs and making a scene. Then she opened up the phonebook and began calling domestic violence shelters and told me I should go there. That was the *best* advice his mother ever gave me; I only wished I had taken it.

I felt isolated in a way that I had never felt before, and I knew at that second that I was on this journey alone; his parents would never help me again. I did not expect, however, when I finally had the courage to stand up and stop the abuse, that his parents would fund Preston's criminal defense team to keep him out of jail. Preston went back into another inpatient psychiatric facility for treatment. I can still remember pushing the baby carriage through the hospital but not being allowed to enter the locked ward where Daddy lived. *How did I come to this?* I wondered. *Bringing my daughter to visit her dad in this place; being married to a man committed to an insane asylum. Will this nightmare ever end?*

The Quiet Woman

*P*reston did not allow me to speak for three years. If I had something I wanted to say, I had to write it down, and if Preston thought it was worthy of discussion, he would allow me to talk to him about it. I was so lonely. I was not permitted to have friends or speak to anyone without his permission. I could not wear makeup or dress nicely unless we were going out in public together—in that case, I was painted to perfection and paraded around like a show pony.

I was not allowed to walk beside Preston; I had to walk behind him. I followed and obeyed. Life was just easier when I listened to him. Preston did not allow me to have a computer. He monitored my phone and even programmed the remote control on our TV in order to monitor the cable. Preston, however, did not lock the PBS station, and this oversight was like a gift from God. I found comfort in watching Dr. Wayne Dyer on PBS. I was reminded of the lessons I learned from Louise Hay, years before, when I was modeling in Taipei, and all of the things I had already overcome. I was inspired by the love coming from Dr. Wayne Dyer's voice. His compassionate nature motivated me to continue fighting for my life one more day. His energy would radiate across my TV screen and fill up the darkness of my soul and my broken home with thoughts of "unlimited possibility."

I would frantically take notes and secretly dream that I too might know joy again. I wondered what my life would have been like if I had been born into his family instead of mine, and I wept. My spirit was so broken that I was just a shell of human being. I was existing but not living. I was breathing to die. Preston forbade me from watching PBS and reading Dr. Dyer's books. He said I was becoming more rebellious, but I think Preston was jealous of everything and everyone that took my attention away from him. He tore up my notes, took my driver's license, took all of the money in my wallet, beat me, and then locked me out of the house. I had to get back inside—my daughter was still in there.

One night, something changed. I could usually tell just before Preston was about to lose control, and I would pick up our baby girl and run into another room. He would regularly chase me around the house and kick down the doors where we were hiding. I would always whisper, "Don't listen, don't listen, don't listen," over and over again in our daughter's ear, trying to soothe her fear of what was going to happen to Mommy next. On this night, however, I did not run. I stayed in the kitchen, and our daughter ran to me instead. She held onto my knees as Preston came closer to us, screaming obscenities. I bent down, looked my daughter in the eyes, and said something very different. I said, "Never let anyone do this to you." She replied, "Mama, why do you?"

Catholic or Bust

I was not allowed to pray to my God anymore. Preston said I had to become Catholic because I was dirty. Father Jack was the family priest. Father Jack spent his summers with us in Maui and spent holidays in our home. Preston's parents built Father Jack's opulent church and the lavish Catholic school too. I made an appointment to see Father Jack and carefully answered his questions. I foolishly felt safe and began to cry. I opened up and told Father Jack how Preston treated me. Father Jack shook his head and then changed the subject.

I felt like I had crossed an invisible line, and there was no going back. My secret was exposed. Father Jack's eyes weighed heavy with judgment, and I felt his self-righteousness silently curse my existence. This priest taught me a valuable lesson: I learned that no one could hide behind God and allow evil to continue in the name of profit and still be considered holy in my eyes.

Nevertheless, I obeyed Preston and registered for Right of Christian Initiation Classes for Adults. I had my First Communion when I was carrying our second child, but the abuse continued. I spent years crying in Father Jack's office, asking for prayer and praying to die.

~

I made Preston angry. I'd asked him to hold our darling son while I went downstairs to help our daughter with a project for school. Preston lunged toward me, screaming as I held our newborn son, and then punched a hole in the wall beside my head and spit in my face. When he took his fist out of the wall, he used his other hand to shove us to the floor. I lost my balance, and we fell down the stairs. When I opened my eyes, I was lying at the bottom of the stairs with the baby in my arms, and our little girl was standing over me, screaming, "Mama, make him stop!"

Preston chased us into the foyer and kicked in the china cabinet. "Look what you made me do, bitch!" Preston shouted. "Why couldn't you just shut the fuck up? What's wrong with you, cunt? You better clean this place up before I get back." And then he stormed out and slammed the door. I called our designer, Katie, for a quote on replacing the custom china cabinet and began to cry. I was not allowed to have friends, so our designers were the closest thing to friendship I had, even though they worked for Preston.

Katie was concerned and came over right away. She could not believe what she walked into and ran back to her car to get the camera. She took pictures of the holes in the wall, the broken furniture, and me. She was worried for our safety and made me promise that I would see a lawyer for advice. The next morning, I made an appointment for the following week with the meanest-looking attorney I could find. I brought copies of Katie's pictures, as well as drawings our daughter had made of me lying on the ground, missing teeth, with Preston standing above me. I cried during my consultation, and the lawyer said I was not ready to file for divorce. He advised me to keep the pictures and drawings in a safe place and wait another year to file. He told me that long-term marriages were those that lasted more than ten years, and if I could make it to the ten-year mark, Preston would have to pay me lifetime alimony. I never wanted to end up back on the street, so waiting another year seemed like a logical decision. The lawyer said to just make the best out of a bad situation and know that in the end, it would benefit me and the children.

~

*W*e bought a lavish beach house and renewed our wedding vows on our ten-year anniversary. I thought that perhaps if we changed locations and rededicated ourselves to one another, Preston would be happy and not hurt me anymore. He always wanted to live beside the sea. I figured a fresh start would benefit everyone … but I was wrong. Preston was really trying to become a better husband and father. He was sober and going to counseling regularly, but he still was abusive. He was trying to use his words more than his body, and I applauded his efforts. He even periodically allowed me to speak to him without a prior written proposal.

On what was to become my night of eternal regret, we stood beside each other in the kitchen of our new home, looking at the pier and reflecting on our struggles. Preston was sorry. Although his words did not display sorrow, his eyes filled with tears, which spoke volumes to my heart. I thought about the divorce lawyer and my hidden photographs and files, and I felt deceptive. I took Preston's hand and led him into the office. I opened up the phonebook and showed him the picture of the lawyer I had seen a year earlier. Preston was shocked that I had considered leaving him. I went upstairs and returned with one file of pictures and drawings from our daughter. Preston began to cry and asked if I had any others. I went back upstairs and brought down five more stacks of terror. As a token of my love and dedication, I offered

Preston all six stacks of documentation. We stood in the office, shredding them together, and then made love.

And I knew in that instant that I had just made the *biggest mistake of my life.*

~

*T*wo months later, Preston said I was crazy, too hard to control, and only good to fuck. He said I needed to go to the doctor and get medicated, or he would leave me. Preston told me exactly what to say, and I obeyed. I did not want to be a single mother with two kids. I was more frightened of the unknown than his consistent rage. The doctor prescribed several medications—one to sleep, one to relax, and one for sadness. I was hoping Preston would be happy now, but he was not. He yelled at me for not filling the prescriptions before I got home, and he made me drive to the pharmacy in the rain with two small children. When I returned home, Preston called me a "fuckin' retard" and said he had me just where he wanted me.

I was confused, but Preston quickly clarified the situation, saying, "Bitch, if you ever leave me now, I will take the kids, and you won't have a leg to stand on. I call the shots, cunt! It's over when I say it's over. Got it? These meds are for crazy bitches like you, stupid fuck. No judge in his right mind would ever let you have the kids over me! I'm a fuckin' prince. I have more money than God. You don't have shit, cunt! No family, no money, nada! You're fucked, retard!"

And I believed him.

Hey Bully, Enough Already!

*W*e did not have a prenuptial agreement. I waived my right to everything in my divorce—the houses, the trust funds, inheritance, educational decision-making rights for our children, health insurance, and even my lifetime alimony. I was so scared of Preston that I did not want to fight him in court. I gave him everything he wanted. Instead of alimony, he offered to let the children and me live in one of his properties for five years—half the length of the marriage—and pay for my education.

Furthermore, if we did not move out by the end of the fifth year, we would be evicted, and I would be responsible for covering all of Preston's legal fees for the eviction. Focusing on school was my ticket out of impending homelessness. Preston purchased a rundown condo, with pet feces- and urine-stained carpet and purple, green, and turquoise walls. He refused to allow me to remove the carpet from the previous owners and said I deserved to live in something that smelled like shit. The walls were so loud it was constantly overstimulating for the children and me, but I was not allowed to paint the walls a neutral color either.

As I soon discovered, the smell of the carpet and color of the walls wasn't the biggest problem with the condo. According to the state of California, the condo was contaminated with 1,963 Aspergillus/Penicillium fungal spores, a dangerous level, as an indoor concentration higher than 750 spores in an indoor environment placed it in the "mold-contaminated" category. Both of our children suffer from asthma and had difficulty breathing. Our daughter had five episodes of anaphylactic shock that landed her in the emergency room, but still, no mold remediation was performed while we lived there.

No repairs were performed at all during our time in the condo; we did not have a working stove for over two years. As far as Preston's covering my educational expenses, he paid for me to attend a trade school and a few classes at a local junior college. He said trade school was all I was worth. The judge said Preston had fulfilled his obligation to cover my educational expenses. Preston's parents were funding his Beverly Hills legal team, as usual, but this time they were burying me alive. Preston even had Father Jack and the principal from the private school his parents built as witnesses of his "upstanding character."

I hired a lawyer from a referral at church, which was a big mistake! I found out too late that she worked for Preston too! She even testified against me in court on behalf of my ex-husband, saying I was lazy. She was the same lawyer who advised me to waive everything in my divorce and agree to all of Preston's requests.

My children and I live in a five-hundred-square-foot, one-bedroom apartment. We're on welfare, as my time is spent in speaking on domestic violence panels, volunteering at a local shelter, and putting myself through school. Thankfully, I have an amazing attorney today who cannot be monetarily seduced by Preston.

I focused on my goals and did not let Preston distract me from reaching them. I graduated cum laude, after three years, with my bachelor's degree in psychology, with course concentrations in biopsychology and cognitive neuroscience and double minors in sociology and gerontology. I was on the Dean's List and received an Outstanding Achievement award, Phi Beta Delta international honors, and Psi Chi national honors. I later obtained my master's degree in gerontology, with concentrations in complementary medicine and counseling, with Sigma Phi Omega honors at USC.

I'm grateful that I qualified for loans to fund my graduate and undergraduate studies to help get us out of poverty. I look toward my $130,000 debt with love and admiration. I will succeed. I will rise above this oppression and continue to share my experiences with those who still suffer in silence. California Child Support Services has taken my case and are requiring my ex-husband to pay his back child support.

Even though he has trust funds and his family lives in opulence, Preston claims to be too poor to pay the court-ordered $1,000 per month in child support, and he continually refuses to disclose his bank accounts. While Preston and his family frequent country clubs, my children and I frequent soup kitchens. The abuse continues; it's just transcended into another form: financial abuse.

Although we struggle for the most basic necessities, I have compassion in my heart and forgiveness in my soul. Hate and bitterness are foreign to my being. I *am* Hope Concorida, and I am still standing!

In Conclusion

I would like to end this book by sending love and gratitude in your direction. Thank you for joining me on my journey of self-discovery and enlightenment. Always remember, the world is as beautiful as you see and say it is. And my world is absolutely pristine!

I will leave you with the words I share at the end of every Survivor talk. They were written by Mother Teresa and are engraved on the walls of her home for unwanted children in Calcutta, India.

~

*P*eople are often unreasonable, irrational, and self-centered. Forgive them anyway.

If you are kind, people may accuse you of selfish, ulterior motives. Be kind anyway.

If you are successful, you will win some unfaithful friends and some genuine enemies. Succeed anyway.

If you are honest and sincere, people may deceive you. Be honest and sincere anyway.

What you spend years creating, others could destroy overnight. Create anyway.

If you find serenity and happiness, some may be jealous. Be happy anyway.

The good you do today will often be forgotten. Do good anyway.

Give the best you have, and it will never be enough. Give your best anyway.

In the final analysis, it is between you and God. It was never between you and them anyway.

Inspiration

"Don't let your throat tighten with fear. Take sips of breath all day and night, before death closes your mouth" (Rumi).

"How people treat you is their karma; how you react is yours" (Dr. Wayne Dyer).

"I leave you free to be yourself, to think your thoughts, to indulge your taste, follow your inclinations, behave in any way that you decide is to your liking" (Anthony de Mello).

"May the vision that so many mystic masters of all traditions have had, of a future world free of cruelty and horror, where humanity can live in the ultimate happiness of the nature of mind, come, through our efforts, to be realized" (Sogyal Rinpoche).

"The intricacies of action are very hard to understand. Therefore, one should know properly what action is, what forbidden action is, and what inaction is" (Bhagavad Gita).

"Give evil nothing to oppose, and it will disappear by itself" (Tao Te Ching).

"Real happiness can stand the challenge of outer experiences. When you can bear the crucifixions of others' wrongs against you and still return love and forgiveness; and when you can't keep that Divine inner peace intact despite all painful thrusts of outer circumstance, then you shall know this happiness" (Paramahansa Yogananda).

"Spiritual achievements are the consummation of holy aspirations" (James Allen).

"The naive mysticism of your Magical Child has expanded into a reflexive mysticism of the adult. You feel a oneness with all creation. You are aware that separation is an illusion" (John Bradshaw).

"I honor the place in you where the entire universe resides. I honor the place in you of love, of light, of truth, of peace. I honor the place within you, where if you are in that place in you and I am in that place in me, there is only one of us" (*namaste* defined by Ram Dass).

"As I walked out the door toward the gate that would lead to my freedom, I knew if I didn't leave my bitterness and hatred behind, I'd still be in prison. Do not judge me by my successes; judge me by how many times I fell down and got back up again" (Nelson Mandela).

"We think sometimes that poverty is only being hungry, naked and homeless. The poverty of being unwanted, unloved and uncared for is the greatest poverty" (Mother Teresa).

"I believe that unarmed truth and unconditional love will have the final word in reality. This is why right, temporarily defeated, is stronger than evil triumphant" (Martin Luther King Jr.).

"I am loved" (Louise Hay).

Resources

The Los Angeles Homeless Services Authority
213-683-3333

Laura's House Domestic Violence Hotline
866-498-1511

National Domestic Violence Hotline
800-799-SAFE (7233)

National Suicide Prevention Lifeline
800-273-TALK (8255)

National Child Abuse Hotline
800-4-A-CHILD (422-4453)

National Runaway Switchboard
800-RUNAWAY (786-2929)

Rape, Abuse and Incest National Network (RAINN)
800-656-HOPE (4673)